THE DOCTRINE OF RELATION IN HEGEL

RELATION IN HEGEL

The Doctrine of Relation in Hegel

Kevin Wall

B
2949
.R28
W34
1983

Copyright © 1983 by
University Press of America,™ Inc.
P.O. Box 19101, Washington, D.C. 20036

All rights reserved

Printed in the United States of America

Library of Congress Cataloging in Publication Data

Wall, Kevin Albert.
  Relation in Hegel.

  Reprint. Originally published: The doctrine of
relation in Hegel. [Oakland, Calif.?] : Albertus Magnus
Press, [1963?]
  Thesis--University of Fribourg.
  Bibliography: p.
  1. Hegel, Georg Wilhelm Friedrich, 1770-1831.
2. Relation (Philosophy)--History. I. Title.
B2949.R28W34 1983   193   82-23775
ISBN 0-8191-2976-3 (pbk.)

ERRATA

p. 6, line 18, for "bestimnte" read "bestimmte"
p. 7, line 20, for "bestimnte" read "bestimmte"
p. 18, line 29, for "far completely" read "far from completely"
p. 19, line 15, for "wihout" read "without"
p. 35, line 3, drop the second "With" and line 5, for "constitues" read "constitutes"
p. 38, line 36, for "which its supports." read "which it supports."
p. 39, line 26, for "which it units" read "which it unites"
p. 47, line 5, for "quantitiative" read "quantitative"
p. 48, line 14, for "smiliarity" read "similarity"
p. 49, line 1, for "reilation" read "relation"
p. 51, line 25, for "os" read "as"
p. 53, line 33, for "consideraing" read "considering"
p. 60, line 17, for "destroy Hegel" read "destroy. Hegel"
p. 73, line 24, for "possible" read "possibly"
p. 74, line 22, for "it does away" read "but it does away"
p. 75, line 20, for "casual" read "causal"
p. 77, line 13, for "let" read "led"
p. 78, line 5, for "considened" read "considered"
p. 80, line 18, for "Aristotalian" read "Aristotelian" and line 21, for "scepticism" read "skepticism"
p. 81, line 7, for "taht" read "that" and line 28, for "real Although" read "real, although"
p. 83, line 18, for "quailties" read "qualities"
p. 86, line 22, for "His notion of how they are relational." read "his notion of how they are relational. But Bradley says:"
p. 93, line 24, for "Grégoine" read "Grégoire" and for "done," read "done." and for "that" read "That"
p. 94, line 9, for "quality" read "quantity"
p. 98, line 13, for "Helegian" read "Hegelian"

ACKNOWLEDGEMENTS

The author would like to thank the publishers for their kind permission to reprint quotations from the following books:

Philosophy, by Bertrand Russell. Used by permission of the publishers, George Allen and Unwin, Ltd.

Mysticism and Logic, by Bertrand Russell. Used by permission of the publishers, George Allen and Unwin, Ltd.

Philosophical Studies, by John McTaggart. Used by permission of the publishers, Edward Arnold, Ltd.

Essays on Truth and Reality, by F. H. Bradley. Used by permission of the publishers, Oxford University Press.

Logic, by Bernard Bosanquet. Used by permission of the publishers, Oxford University Press.

The Philosophy of Hegel, by W. T. Stace. Used by permission of the publishers, Dover Publications, Inc.

INTRODUCTION

The purpose of this work is to study the significance of the doctrine of relation in Hegel—how he conceives of this category of being, and how he uses it to structure reality and thought. Such an investigation needs no lengthy justification, since it deals with a fundamental element in one of the most influential of modern systems of philosophy. Yet, for this very reason one might think it pointless on the ground that it must surely have been made already. This, in fact, is not the case, surprising as it may seem. The function of relation in the thought of Hegel has not yet been studied with the thoroughness and precision which it demands. Modern commentators, as Coreth remarks, have not, with the possible exception of Bradley, given it sufficient attention.[1] The reason for this is apparently their impoverished notion concerning it. In modern philosophy, the problem of relation has scarcely been posed. And the little that is known about this peculiar category of being is all too insufficient to deal with its richness in Hegel. This is not the case, in Coreth's opinion, for scholasticism. Its notion of relation is subtle and well-developed. This permits such a thinker as Grégoire, who approaches Hegel from a scholastic background, to treat of his dialectic with unusual flexibility and to provide new and illuminating insights into it.[2]

The historical background to the research on this problem is therefore relatively meager. Aside from Bradley, there is no one among the post-Hegelians who really comes to grips with it. Many mention it in passing but few attempt seriously to deal with it.

Not even Bradley, in fact, does this. He treats only of the generic nature of relation and from this draws all of his conclusions. This is the principle from which he deduces the basic difficulties of the Hegelian system: the problem of Consciousness, Intelligence, Will and Personality in the Absolute; the problem of the unity and plurality

---

[1] E. Coreth, *Das dialektische Sein in Hegels Logik*, p. 24.
[2] *Ibidem*.

of being. And it is the source from which he forms his own conclusions concerning these problems.

He reasons in general from a generic and univocal notion of relation. He does not consider its analogous *ratio* and its many distinct forms. As a result, his conclusions are so extreme and unreal as to provoke the strongest reaction.[3] This has led many to consider them as "mystical" rather than rational.[4]

Yet, if Bradley did nothing else, he at least showed the crucial significance of relation for Hegelian thought. And this result has taken root among subsequent commentators. Not qualities, they agree, but relations are the prime problem of the dialectic.[5]

This paper does not pretend to solve such a weighty problem but only to study it. The sheer difficulty of the subject in itself, let alone in this most difficult of philosophers, makes modesty imperative, if no other motive were available. But the writer is reconciled to this limitation by Aristotle's dictum that, although no one adds very much to truth on his own initiative, the little bit he does add, when totalled up with all that has been discovered by others, results in a considerable body of knowledge.[6]

I wish to express my gratitude to the Very Reverend Joseph Fulton, O.P., former Provincial of the Province of the Holy Name, for his kindness to me in providing the opportunity for this study, as well as to the Very Reverend Joseph Agius, O.P., present Provincial, for his encouragement and for the extension of sufficient time to bring the work to a conclusion. I wish also to express my deep appreciation to Father I. M. Bochenski, O.P., of the University of Fribourg, for suggesting the subject of the study and for patiently reading and discussing it with me in the course of its development. This help was invaluable. I am also deeply grateful for the reading of the manuscript by Father N. Luyten, O.P., Professor at the University, and former Rector, whose criticisms proved most helpful in the preparation of the manuscript for publication.

---

[3] E. Gellner, *Words and Things*, p. 71.
[4] McTaggart, *Philosophical Studies*, pp. 46, 47.
[5] E. Coreth, *op. cit.*, p. 23.
[6] *Metaphysics* II, 1, 993 b 2.

TABLE OF CONTENTS

INTRODUCTION vii

I. THE DEFINITION OF THE CATEGORY OF RELATION   1
   A. Hegel's Notion of Definition 1
   B. Hegel's Definition of Relation 2
       In the Philosophical Propaedeutics 2
       In the Science of Logic 5
       In the Encyclopedia of 1817 8
       In the Encyclopedia of 1827 9
   C. Comparison of the Definitions 11
   D. Genus and Specifying Differences 13
       The Relation of Whole and Part 14
       The Relation of Force and Its Manifestations . . 14
       The Relation of Inner and Outer 16

II. THE NATURE OF APPEARANCE 19
   A. In the Phenomenology of Mind 19
   B. In the Logic 27

III. THE BROADER NOTION OF RELATION IN HEGEL . 33
   A. The Presence of the Broader Notion in Hegel . . . 36
       In the Category of Quality: Becoming . . . 36
       In the Category of Quality: Determined Being . 41
       In the Category of Quantity 44
       In the Category of Measure 45
       In the Category of Essence 45
   B. The Division of Relation in the Broader Sense . . . 46
       The Division in Itself 46
       A Scholastic Interpretation of It 47
          Of Position and Negation 47
          Of Reconciliation 48
          Of Quantitative Relation 49
          Of Essential Relation 49
          Of Absolute Relation 49
          Summary 50

IV. THE FUNDAMENTAL RELATIONS 51

A. How Hegel Conceives of Position 52
B. How Hegel Conceives of Negation 56
C. How Hegel Conceives of Reconciliation . . . 58
  - The Existence of This Relation 58
  - The Nature of This Relation 58
  - The Importance of This Relation 60
  - A Scholastic Interpretation 60
  - Confirmation by Criticism 64

D. Summary 66

V. THE TREATMENT OF THIS DOCTRINE BY LATER PHILOSOPHERS 68

A. Introduction 68
  - The Importance of the Doctrine 68
  - The Inadequacy of Their Treatment of It . . 69
  - The Result of This Inadequacy 70
  - Bradley's Contribution 72

B. Bradley's Doctrine on the Structure of Experience . . 72
  - Relation and the Beginning of Experience . . . 72
    - That the Beginning is One 72
    - Against Pluralism 74
      - The Position in Itself 74
      - Bradley's Reply 75
      - The Crucial Point: External Relations . . 77
    - Summary 80
    - Criticism 80
  - Relation and Transcendance of Experience . . 81
    - Relation as Effecting Transcendance . . . 81
    - Difficulties of the Position 83
    - Criticism 84
  - Termination of Experience in the Absolute . . 84
    - No Relation in the Absolute 85
    - The Heart of the Argument 86
    - Objection Against It 86

C. Summary and Criticism 87
  - Summary 87
  - Criticism 87

VI. SUMMARY AND CRITICISM 90
   A. Summary of the Hegelian Doctrine on Relation . . 90
      The Category of Relation 91
      Other Relations 91
      Reference (Beziehung) 91
   B. Systematization of the Doctrine 93
      Abstract Ratio of Relation 93
      Specific Ratios of Relation 93
        Primary Relation 93
        Secondary Relations 93
   C. Identification of These Relations in A Scholastic Context 93
      Rational Relations 93
      Real Relations 94
        Predicamental Relations 94
        Transcendental Relations 94
      Mixed Relations 95
   D. Difficulty of the Hegelian Doctrine 97
   E. Interpretation of Reconciliation 98
   F. Criticism of the Doctrine 98

BIBLIOGRAPHY 101

CHAPTER I

THE DEFINITION OF THE CATEGORY OF RELATION

A. Hegel's Notion of Definition

Hegel distinguishes two different conceptions of definition. The first regards it as a rational formality, external to the thing defined; the second, as an expression of the inner constitutive principles of the latter. This second conception is the one which he approves and attempts to achieve.

Thus, in the *Phenomenology of Mind*, while discussing the division of electricity into positive and negative, he tells us that if we hold this division to pertain to the definition of the subject, then we mean that it is the concept and the essence (Wesen) of the latter.[1] This, therefore, is what we will understand by the Hegelian definition of the category of relation. It is not a merely rational construction, but the expression of the ontological structure of relation.

Hegel's definition is built up out of the elements of all thought and reality. He objects to the inverse conception whereby it is made, as it were, the pre-supposition and the beginning of thought. In the *History of Philosophy* he criticizes Spinoza for this false notion by reason of which he made philosophy, in imitation of mathematics, follow from certain initial definitions.[2] These latter were thus conceived of as purely universal determinations (allgemeine Bestimmungen) and so, on the whole, as merely formal ones.[3] This conception was the essential defect (das Mangelhafte) in the phil-

---

[1]*Phänomenologie des Geistes*, Gl. 2, p. 125. Citations of the works of Hegel will be from the edition of Glockner, and will be identified by the name of the work, the volume in the edition, and the page in the volume.
[2]*Geschichte der Philosophie* III, Gl. 19, p. 384 ff.
[3]*Ibidem*.

osophy of Spinoza.[4] It is not a defect in mathematics where the point of departure is a rational presupposition (eine Voraussetzung)— a line, a point and so forth. But it is a defect in philosophy where the point of departure is the ontological truth of the thing considered. In this case, the determinations of the object must be drawn from its own nature.[5]

Thus, for Hegel, definition expresses the genus (Gattung) of a singular or particular object as its universal being (allgemeines Wesen) and its particular determinateness (besondere Bestimmtheit) as that which makes it specifically this thing. So understood it reduces the complexity of the determinations of intued being (des angeschauten Daseins) to its simplest elements, performing, in this, one of the necessary functions of thought and constituting a special movement in synthetic knowledge. The simplest elements which it uses for this are also the principles of the object in itself. Definition is not, therefore, a purely formal disposition of determinations external to the structure of the defined thing.[6]

Again, in the *Philosophische Propädeutik*, which he wrote as a program for class lectures at Nuremburg, Hegel tells us the same: definition is the expression of the genus and the particular differentiating principle of an object.[7] It posits the object as a singular,[8] and gives the fundamental principles through which it is such.[9]

B. Hegel's Definition of Relation

With this in mind, we may now consider the diverse definitions of relation which Hegel gives in his works. Although this is not crucial, we shall take them in their chronological order.

1. In the *Philosophical Propaedeutics*

In the *Philosophical Propaedeutics*, which was written during the period from 1808 to 1816, when he was director of the Aegidiengymnasium at Nuremburg, Hegel gives the following definition of relation:

---

[4] *Ibidem.*
[5] *Ibidem.*
[6] *Philosophische Propädeutik*, Gl. 3, p. 164.
[7] *Ibidem.*
[8] *Ibidem.*
[9] *Ibidem.*

Relation (Verhältniss) is a reference (Beziehung) of two sides (Seiten) one to the other, which sides have partly an indifferent (gleichgültiges) existence, and partly an existence one through the other (jede durch die andere) in the unity of determination (Bestimmtseins).[10]

In this definition, the genus is *reference* (Beziehung). One would be inclined to translate this word itself as "relation" but since this would make the definition logically defective—since it would then define the subject by itself—we may distinguish it at least verbally by the word "reference". Later we shall see the deeper significance of this semantic problem. For the moment we shall note only that relation is defined as a *sort* of *reference*. Its particularity is then determined through its constitutive principles: its *two sides* (Seiten). This suggests that within the genus of reference there is an opposed sort which is not constituted of two sides. It also suggests that there is some reason why relation should *have* two sides. Hegel gives this reason explicitly in the *Logic*,[11] but since he does not concern himself with it in the present text, for the moment, we shall not consider it.

The definition then goes on to characterize the mode of existence of the opposed terms in the reference. It is an existence (Bestehen) which partly is independent and partly dependent. In so far as it is independent, the two sides are indifferent one to the other.[12] In so far as it is dependent, they are tied one to the other, so that one cannot exist without the other, and both coexist in the unity (Einheit) of mutual determination (Bestimmtseins).

Relation, so defined, is not merely a general category of objectivity, but a conditioned one. This is indicated in the final words: *Bestimmtsein*. Relation involves determinations (Bestimmungen).[13] It is therefore conditioned (bedingt).[14] The first of these conditions is, precisely because it is first, *immediate*.[15] Combined with the generic ratio of relation, this produces the immediately conditioned relation or that of the *part* and the *whole*.[16] When another condition is added (a condition which is therefore mediated) a new sort of relation arises:

---

[10] *Ibidem*, p. 125.
[11] *Logik* I, Cl. 4, p. 639.
[12] *Philosophische Propädeutik*, Cl. 3, 125.
[13] *Logik* I, Cl. 4, p. 641.
[14] *Ibidem*.
[15] *Ibidem*.
[16] *Ibidem*.

that of *force* (Kraft) and its *manifestation* (Aüsserung).[17] This new relation of its very nature establishes a distinction of inner and outer and therefore gives rise to the relation of the *inner* and the *outer* (Innern und Aüssern).[18]

The import of this division and of the definition upon which it depends cannot be fully grasped unless the treatment is situated in the context of the *Propaedeutics* as a whole. This is, in fact, suggested by the differentiating principle "of two sides," which can only occur at a determined position in the total system of the *Propaedeutics*. And in this way that position determines its meaning.

The *Propaedeutics* is divided into three Cursus, the first of these for a lower, the second for an intermediate, and the third for an upper Class.[19] The Cursus for the lower class is entirely taken up with ethical doctrine. That of the middle class is concerned with the *Phenomenology of Mind* and with *Logic*. The Cursus for the upper class contains the logical doctrine of the *Begriff* (concept) and an outline of a philosophical encyclopedia. Of these three, it is the second which contains the definition of relation.

It is given in the second division of the second Cursus, that is to say, in the treatise on Logic. Hegel divides this treatise into three parts. The first is concerned with Being (Seyn); The second, with Essence (Wesen); and the third, with the Concept (Begriff).[20] Relation is determined to pertain to Essence (Wesen). It thus belongs immediately to Essence, mediately to Being, and, as a presupposition to Concept.

The realm of Essence is itself divided into three parts: that of Essence in itself; that of Appearance or Phenomenon (Erscheinung) and that of Actuality (Wirklichkeit).[21] Relation is then assigned its position in Appearance. It is therefore posterior to Essence in itself and prior to Actuality.

This position serves to determine its genus (Gattung)[22] more immediately than that suggested by "reference" (Beziehung). It i

---

[17]*Ibidem.*
[18]*Ibidem.*
[19]Glockner edition, Volume 3.
[20]*Philosophische Propädeutik*, Gl. 3, p. 138.
[21]*Ibidem*, p. 127.
[22]*Ibidem*, p. 163.

therefore related to the former as the proximate genus to the remote or as the immediate to the ultimate. But since a further development of this thought would take us beyond the context of the *Propaedeutics*, we will carry it no further but pass on to the definition of relation given in the *Science of Logic*.

2. The Definition of Relation in the *Science of Logic*

The *Science of Logic*, which was written during the same period as the *Propaedeutics*,—that is to say, while Hegel was at Nuremberg—and which was intended as an independent and thorough exposition of his logical doctrine rather than as an outline for lectures in class—presents the following definition:

> The truth of appearance (Erscheinung) is the essential relation (wesentliche Verhältniss).[23]

We may invert the order of predication in order to make the relation itself the subject and then restate the proposition: the essential relation is the truth of appearance.

In this definition, the subject is not relation in general but as qualified. It is *essential* relation. This would lead one to believe that other sorts are also recognized by Hegel and that what he calls relation here is simply one of them. This is, in fact, the case. For in treating of the category of Quantity, prior to that of Essence, he mentions another sort of relation (which is not considered to be such in the *Propaedeutics*), namely, *quantitative ratio*, or "*quantitative Verhältniss.*"[24] This, he affirms, is not only *in* a relation (im Verhältniss) but is itself posited as a relation (es selbst ist als Verhältniss gesetzt).[25] Thus, besides an essential relation, he also admits a quantitative one.

Again, in treating of Actuality which immediately follows Appearance in the Logic, he posits a third movement of thought which he calls *Absolute Relation*.[26] This movement, he affirms, is relational because it is distinguished in itself and its moments are its whole totality

---
[23]*Logik* I, Gl. 4, p. 639.
[24]*Ibidem*, p. 393.
[25]*Ibidem*.
[26]*Ibidem*, p. 696.

(Sie ist Verhältniss, weil sie Unterscheiden ist, dessen Momente selbst ihre ganze Totalität sind).[27] Thus we have not only essential relation, but quantitative and absolute.

Let us return again to the definition. It states that essential relation is the truth of appearance (die Wahrheit der Erscheinung), and therefore truth as this manifests itself in appearance. By this, it provides us with a new concept of relation, that of its being a "truth". And it assigns to this new notion the generic place of *reference* (Beziehung) in the text already quoted from the *Philosophical Propaedeutics*.[28] Relation, in that text, was a sort of *reference*; in the *Logic* it is a sort of *truth*.

One might ask whether these two are distinct genera or the same, and, if they are the same, how they can be. These are obviously important questions but we will not stop to consider them here. Rather we will continue to study of the text of the *Logic* in which Hegel further enriches his notion of essential relation.

This relation, he tells us next, contains the determined unity (bestimnte Vereinigung) of Essence (Wesen) and Existence (Existenz).[29] It does so because it is the third movement of Appearance, whose first movement is that of Existence and whose second, that of Phenomenal Being proper.[30] The third movement, in this case must be the assumption of the first two into a higher principle of unity.[31] Thus, Essential Relationship must unify Existence and Phenomenality of Being. But this is to unify Essence (Wesen) and Existence (Existenz). Therefore Essential Relation must unite these two.

Again every higher uniting principle enriches its lower principle with a true infinity of qualification (Bestimmung).[32] But Essential Relation is the higher uniting principle of Essence and Existence. It therefore must so enrich them, or in other words, it must be their determined unity (bestimmte Vereinigung).[33] Moreover, Essential Relation has "sides" (Seiten),[34] that is to say its terms are posited

---
[27] *Ibidem*.
[28] Cf. text, p. 3.
[29] *Logik* I, Gl. 4, p. 639, 140.
[30] *Ibidem*, p. 622 ff.
[31] *Ibidem*, p. 639 ff.
[32] *Ibidem*, p. 157 ff.
[33] *Ibidem*, p. 639.
[34] *Ibidem*, p. 640.

as independent *totalities*.³⁵ To explain this assertion, Hegel uses the notion of Reflection (Reflexion). He tells us:

> Relation has sides (Seiten), because it is reflection (Reflexion) into another (in Anderes).³⁶

If it were not this—let us say, if it were, for example, reflection into itself—it would not have "sides". These, therefore, which are thus so essential an element in the determination of the category of Essential Relation, are *Totalities*, having *Otherness*, which are united by *Reflection*. Thus, they have *unity* in so far as they are reflected upon. And they are "sides" in so far as they are independent totalities.³⁷

This conclusion permits Hegel to develope further the notion of Essential Relation by comparing it with those kinds of reflection-determinations (Reflexions-Bestimmungen) which are likewise reflections into themselves but which *do not* have "sides".³⁸ This is the case for the "Reflexions-Bestimmungen" of the positive and the negative.³⁹ These too turn into themselves only in so far as they turn into their opposites.⁴⁰ But they have no other determniation except that of heir negative unity (ihre negative Einheit).⁴¹ Essential Relation has also the determination of mutually opposed *independent* Totalities.⁴² That is to say, it is determined (bestimnt) by determinations (Bestimmungen) which have also independence or indifferent existence.⁴³

Clearly this situation is in one way quite similar to that of the negative and the positive. For in them too there is opposition (Entgegensetzung).⁴⁴ But there is this difference that in Essential Relation it is the opposition of an "inverted world" (verkehrte Welt)⁴⁵—a topsy-turvey world⁴⁶—since its sides are Totalities (i.e wholes in themselves and, to this extent, completed things) and yet have opposites; and since one or other of the opposites may, for this very

---

³⁵*Ibidem*, p. 639.
³⁶*Ibidem*, p. 639.
³⁷*Ibidem*.
³⁸*Ibidem*, p. 640.
³⁹*Ibidem*.
⁴⁰*Ibidem*.
⁴¹*Ibidem*.
⁴²*Ibidem*.
⁴³*Ibidem*.
⁴⁴*Ibidem*.
⁴⁵*Ibidem*.
⁴⁶Findlay, *Hegel*, p. 94.

reason, take priority and, as it were, rise to the top, inverting the picture of the world. This cannot happen in the opposition of the negative and the positive.[47]

Since the "sides" of an Essential Relation are totalities with opposites, it is therefore relative to a beyond (Jenseits).[48] Each of its sides seems to point to this. But this is mere appearance.[49] For their existence is *not* their own but that of the other.[50]

Essential Relation is thus "broken in itself" (in sich selbst Gebrochenes).[51] For it is divided into independent totalities. But it is also an inner resolution of this division through the unity of itself and its other, for which reason it has independent existence and is essentially reflection into itself.[52] For this reason also it is a whole.[53] This, Hegel tells us, makes it the notion or concept (Begriff) of relation.[54]

3. The Definition of Relation in the *Encyclopedia of 1817*

In the original version of the *Encyclopedia of the Philosophical Sciences*, which was published at Heidelberg in 1817, where he had taken the post of professor,[55] Hegel thus defines relation:

> The existing thing (das Existirende) or the Appearance (Erscheinung) in its determination (in ihre Bestimmtheit) is therefore *relation* (das Verhältniss), which, while remaining one and the same, is the opposition (Entgegensetzung) of independent existences, whose identical reference (identische Beizehung) is that in which alone the distinguished terms (die Unterschiedenen) are what they are.[56]

The language of this definition is somewhat difficult but its confusions can be easily cleared up by separating out its distinct affirmations.

The first of these is that relation is the *existing thing* (das Existirende). This defines it in terms of existence, and, specifically, that of the existing thing, or of the concrete reality whose nature

---
[47] *Logik* I, p. 640.
[48] *Ibidem.*
[49] *Ibidem.*
[50] *Ibidem.*
[51] *Ibidem.*
[52] *Ibidem.*
[53] *Ibidem.*
[54] *Ibidem.*
[55] Ueberweg, *History of Philosophy*, volume II, p. 237.
[56] *Encyclopädie*, Gl. 6, p. 80.

then determines as "appearance in its determination" (Erscheinung in ihrer Bestimmtheit). Thus, it conceives relation to be *appearance in determination*.

The second affirmation is that relation is a unity and does not cease to be a unity ("while remaining one and the same . . ."). But, it is unity which contains opposition. For this reason it may be said to *be* an opposition (Entgegensetzung). It is therefore a *unity* which is at the same time an *opposition*, i.e. a unity sustained in an identical reference (identische Beziehung). But this identical reference contains opposed and independent existences (selbstständige Existenzen). Therefore it is only because this latter *is* one and identical that the independent existences can be distinct and can be what they are at all.[57]

The first affirmation—relation is the existing thing—gives Essence (Wesen) as the genus and Existence as the differentiation. The qualification—that relation is appearance in its determination—gives Appearance as the genus and Determination (Bestimmung) as the difference. The second affirmation—that relation is an opposition—gives a genus which is common to other than essential relations (to negation and position also, as we have already seen).[58] The qualification that relation is nevertheless a *unity* may be considered the predication of a property (Eigenschaft) or it may again be considered as itself definitory.

At all events it is clear that the text adds no new generic or differentiating element. Its genera are all ones which we have seen given before: that relation is appearance or pertains to appearance; that it is opposition; that it is unity. These conceptions therefore offer no peculiar difficulty.

4. The Definition of Relation in the *Encyclopedia of 1827*

In the second edition of the *Encyclopedia*, published in 1827 while he was teaching in Berlin, and much enlarged through additions (Zusätze) and remarks (Anmerkungen),[59] Hegel offers this notion of Essential Relation.[60]

---
[57] *Ibidem.*
[58] *Logik* I, Gl. 4, p. 640.
[59] *Encyclopädie*, Gl. 8.
[60] *Ibidem*, p. 305.

Essential relation is the determined (bestimmte), totally universal (ganz allgemeine) mode (Weise) of appearance. Everything which exists stands in a relationship and this relationship is the truth of every existence. The existing thing is therefore not an abstraction for itself but something only in another, but in this other it is a reference to itself (Beziehung auf sich) and the relation is the unity of the reference to itself and the reference to another.[61]

This text is rich in content and therefore well worth detailed analysis.

The first affirmation which it makes is this: that Essential Relation is a determined mode of appearance. This suggests that we should distinguish *appearance, mode* of appearance, and *determination* of mode of appearance, thereby seeming to make the *mode* different from determination. This cannot, however, be the case since it is clear that *mode* is to *appearance* as *determination* is to the *determined* and, therefore, that it is not essentially distinct from the latter. The enriched definition, to which the text is an addition, clearly corroborates this conclusion, as does the definition of the earlier edition of the *Encyclopedia*. Both affirm that relation is appearance in its determination (Bestimmtheit). It therefore follows that mode (Weise) is simply another way of regarding determination. The appearance, with its determination, has a mode of being.

The second affirmation of the text is this: Essential Relation is a totally universal mode of appearance. This statement is immediately elaborated upon. It means that everything which exists has existence through its being contained in a relationship outside of which it cannot exist. It cannot, therefore, be an abstraction (taken away from the relationship) or a thing *for itself*, but must have being in itself and reference to itself (Beziehung auf sich) only in so far as being by reference or relation to another. Relation, therefore, is its *truth* and is, moreover, the unity of reference to itself and to another.[62]

The definitory notions which this text posits with respect to relation are those given at its beginning and end. The beginning repeats what we have already seen: that relation *is* by reference to Appearance (here the text uses *Erscheinen* rather than *Erscheinung*).[63] It is the determinate and totally universal mode of Appearance, that is, o

---

[61] *Ibidem.*
[62] *Ibidem.*
[63] *Ibidem.*

Existence. This adds to what we have already seen only the notion of the *universality* of the mode.

The definitory notion given at the end of the text is particularly interesting since it shows Hegel's capacity to reduce his thoughts step by step to a precise and clear form. This is all too often lacking in his earlier works where he is still not completely at ease with his theme, as in the well known case of the *Phenomenology of Mind*, whose obscurities are legendary and whose turgid language has merited the disapproval of generations of students of German literature.

The defining notion is this: that relation is the *unity* of *reference* of a thing to itself and to another. It is "Beziehung auf sich" but at the same time "Beziehung auf Anderes."[64] "Beziehung" is, as it were, the subject. "Einheit" is the form. Relation *is* this latter. It is the unity of a reference which is bilateral.

This conception of it is a theoretical challenge. For it demands, in order that it be understood, that one first understand "Beziehung"; and then that one understand how more than one "Beziehung" can be compounded into a true unity. If one can understand this, then he can grasp the Hegelian concept of relation. If he cannot do so, then this concept must remain obscure for him. The challenge is clear and its terms are precisely exposed.

But, for the moment, let us avoid any further consideration of this matter since our purpose, at this point, is not to set aside every difficulty as it occurs, but to obtain a general idea of the way in which Hegel defines the notion of relation in his various works. This we have now done. And our next obvious step is to compare the results so as to draw a common notion or definition from them.

C. Comparison of the Definitions

The comparison of the definitions reveals immediately that to some extent at least they are not the same. For one thing, their subjects differ. The subject, in the *Philosophical Propaedeutics* and in the *Encyclopedia* of 1827, is not the same as that of the *Logic* and the

[64]*Ibidem.*

Encyclopedia of 1817. In the former the subject is "relation"; in the latter (which occupies the same position in the totality of systematic presentation), it is "essential relation". And although at times these two seem to be used interchangeably, at other times, they do not.

Again, the *generic ratios* are not identical. In one case, it is *reference;* then it is *truth;* then it is *existing thing;* again, it is *determination;* again, *opposition;* again, *reflection;* again, *mode.*

Thus, both in the subject of the definition, and in the generic ratio, there is clearly a difference in the various texts.

On the other hand, there is also an obvious similarity or even identity which runs through the majority of the definitions. For the greater number of them involve either explicit or implicit reference to "appearance". They define relation as a "determination *of appearance*",[65] the *truth of appearance,*[66] the "determined universal mode *of appearance*".[67] In these definitions, the reference to appearance is explicit. In others, it is implicit, as in the case of the definition of relation as an "opposition *of independent existences*"[68] where "existence" is defined in the total context as that which is *constituted through appearance.*[69]

The implicit invocation of "appearance" as an element of definition is not so clear in the *Philosophical Propaedeutics.* There, relation is defined as a "reference of two sides one to the other".[70] In this definition, "reference" (Beziehung) does not necessarily imply "appearance", for there are *Beziehungen* which do not pertain to the order of the phenomenal.[71] But true as this is, the connection between the referential character of relation and the category of Appearance is none the less implicit. The implication lies in the differentiating element "of two sides". For it is only in the category of Appearance that *two sides* properly exist, that is, that otherness in the full sense is had.[72] Thus, implicitly, the differentiating principle "of two sides" contains the defining element "of appearance".

---

[65] Footnote no. 56, p. 8.
[66] Footnote no. 23, p. 5.
[67] Footnote no. 61, p. 10.
[68] Footnote no. 56, p. 8.
[69] Footnote no. 56, p. 8.
[70] Footnote no. 10, p. 3.
[71] *Ibidem.*
[72] Footnote no. 36, p. 7.

There still remains the definition of relation as the "truth of appearance". Its use of "appearance" is obviously not in question; its use of *truth* is. Yet the meaning of this is not difficult to discover. *Truth* means that which constitutes an object giving it structure and being and a place in the hierarchy of beings.[73] Hegel tells us in this definition that, for Appearance Essential Relation does this. It constitutes Appearance. Essence cannot "appear" except through Essential Relation. The truth or entity or structure of the appearance of Essence, therefore, is simply the content of Essential Relation. So again Essential Relation is defined by its order to appearance.

D. The Genus and Specifying Differences of Relation

In the definition of "definition" which Hegel gives in his *Philosophical Propaedeutics* and which we have already cited,[74] he asserts that the genus (Gattung) of the defined thing is its universal being (sein allgemeines Wesen), and that its differentiating principles are determinations of this universal being (die besondere Bestimmtheit dieses Allgemeinen).[75] We have now shown that the *genus* of relation for him is its reference to appearance (it is always "of appearance"). We must still determine what its differentiating principles are.

For clarity we should note that we are seeking the differentiating principles of the genus of relation itself, not those which distinguish relation from *reference* (Beziehung).[76] Relation is distinguished from *reference* by the fact that it has *sides* (Seiten) whereas reference does not of necessity have them.[77] But this distinction does not concern us at the moment. We are now concerned solely with the distinctions which the proper differentiating principles produce in relation itself.

Hegel makes clear to us what these are in each of the texts already studied and he shows, in each case, how they specify relation. The species which thus result are the following.

1. The relation of the Whole and the Part
2. The relation of Force and Manifestation of Force
3. The relation of Inner and Outer.[78]

---

[73]Findlay, *Hegel*, p. 46.
[74]Footnote no. 7, p. 2.
[75]*Ibidem*.
[76]Footnote no. 10, p. 3.
[77]*Ibidem*.
[78]*Logik* I, Gl. 4, p. 641.

1. The Relation of Whole and Part

In the *Philosophical Propaeduetics,* this relationship is defined in the following way:

> The immediately conditioned (unmittelbar bedingt) relation is that of the Whole and its Parts (das des Ganzen und der Theile). The Parts, as something outside of the relation, existing in themselves (für sich Bestehendes), are mere matter (bloss Materien) and to this extent not parts. As parts, they have their determination (Bestimmung) only in the Whole, and it is the Whole which makes them Parts, but, on the other hand, it is the Parts which make the Whole to be a Whole.[79]

It is clear that in this statement the condition (Bedingung) or determination (Bestimmung), which makes relation to exist as *this* rather than as totally undetermined, is that of the Whole and the Parts. This is, therefore, the differentiating principle which, added to the generic *ratio,* determines the inner constitution of this particular relation.

Hegel asserts that it is immediate (unmittelbar). Between it and the generic *ratio* there is no other. In it and through it, therefore, relation manifests itself immediately. It makes parts to be parts and wholes to be whole, and relation to subsist between them in the particular form of Whole and Part.

So again in the *Logic,* he affirms:

> "Essential relation is therefore immediately the relation of Whole and Part."[80]

And in the Encyclopedia, both in the earlier and in the later version he reiterates the same.

2. The Relation of Force and Its Manifestation

Upon the immediately differentiating principle, which establishes the specific relation of the Whole and the Part when added to the generic *ratio* of relation, there follows a second (a mediating one therefore) which establishes another relation: that of Force and its Manifestation. Hegel presents this second principle in the *Philosophical Propaeduetics*: The Whole, as inner active form, is Power

---

[79] *Philosophische Propädeutik,* Gl. 3, p. 126.
[80] *Logik* I, Gl. 4, p. 641.
[81] *Philosophische Propädeutik,* Gl. 3, p. 126.

Here, it is an "inner activity". When this is added to the determination which constitutes Whole as Whole, it produces what he calls Power (Kraft) or Force. He goes on to explain that it does not operate through a matter external to that which is Force (sie hat keine aüssere Materie zu ihrer Bedingung) but rather through the internal matter itself (sondern ist in der Materie selbst).[82] If this is so, what, then, is the conditioning factor of the Force? Hegel answers that it is not in an external matter but only in an external resistance (Anstoss) which provokes its manifestation (*erscheinen*, in this text) by way of sollicitation (Sollicitation).[83] On the other hand, it is itself the manifestation of a Force and therefore itself demands sollicitation to appear.[84]

The differentiating principle which constitutes this relation is presented with great richness of detail and depth of analysis in the *Science of Logic*.[85] There Hegel tells us that Force is the negative unity (negative Einheit) in which the contradiction of the Whole and the Parts is resolved. This contradiction is that whereby the Parts are all that they are by relation to the Whole and the Whole all that it is by relation to them, and thus the existence of one is really the existence of the other.[86] To this situation the relation of Force and its Manifestation brings the differentiation of a higher unification and resolution.[87] This differentiation, then, is that which is added to the immediate condition productive of the Whole-Part relation in order to produce the relation of the Force and Manifestation.

Again, the relation of the Whole and its Parts is on lacking in thought. The relation of Force and its Manifestation is thus differentiated from this by the fact that it adds the quality of thought.[88]

Moreover, he relation of the Whole and the Part is, objectively speaking, a dead, mechanical aggregate (todte, mechanische Aggregat). But that of Force and its Manifestation is a higher return into self (die höhere Rückkehr in sich).[89] The differentiation which it adds is thus that of "return into self".

In sum, then, the differentiating principle constituting this higher relation within the genus of Essential Relation is that of resolution of

---

[82] *Ibidem.*
[83] *Ibidem.*
[84] *Ibidem.*
[85] *Logik* I, G. 4, 648.
[86] *Ibidem.*
[87] *Ibidem.*
[88] *Ibidem.*
[89] *Ibidem.*

contradiction, addition of "thought" and return into self. These three are, in fact, one and the same thing. For contradiction is always resolved by the addition of "thought" or "Begriff" and this latter is essentially "the return into self."[90]

3. The Relation of Inner and Outer

That the relation of Force and its Manifestation is not the final one within the genus of Essential Relation is established by Hegel, in the *Philosophical Propaedeutics*, through the argument that this relation is itself in one sense unconditioned.[91] Now if this is true, it follows that it is determinable. And it follows also that its determination will constitute a new differentiation within the genus and therefore a new relation.

That this is the case Hegel proves in the following way: Force demands for its evocation that it be sollicited by a resistance which is itself an expression of another Force and therefore itself demands sollicitation by a resistance. Therefore Force and Resistance form a mutual condition and being conditioned (Bedingen und Bedingtseyn). But such a situation is itself, taken as a whole, an unconditioned one. Therefore, Force and Resistance form an unconditioned relation, which is to say that Force and its Manifestation do this, since Resistance is simply that which evokes Manifestation.[92]

The precise condition which determines this relation is that of Inner and Outer.[93] This, therefore, constitutes a new principle of differentiation, and is thus the source of a new relation—that of the Inner and Outer.[94]

That which is Inner and that which is Outer (the terms which have themselves one to the other by this relationship) are therefore one and the same thing but seen from different sides.[95] The Inner is the perfection of content-determinations (Inhaltbestimmungen) as condition which themselves have existence.[96] The Outer or Exterior is the reflec

---

[90] *Ibidem.*
[91] *Philosophische Propädautik*, Gl. 3, p. 126.
[92] *Ibidem.*
[93] *Ibidem.*
[94] *Ibidem.*
[95] *Ibidem,* p. 127.
[96] *Ibidem.*

tion (Reflexion) of this same thing, or its unification (Zusammen-nehmen) in the unity of one Whole, which thereby gains existence.[97]

The principle of differentiation, which establishes this relation, is that of the conditioning of the unconditioned relation of Force and its Manifestation. But is it too in some similar way an unconditioned relation so as to give rise to another species within the genus? Hegel asserts that it is not and that what lies beyond it is the dissolution of relation and the emergence of a still higher principle of unity.[98]

He argues to this conclusion in the following way: the distinction between Inner and Outer is, in the last analysis, purely formal.[99] That which is the Inner may be transposed and take the place of the Outer and again the reverse may happen. Thus they are fundamentally one and the same thing. Therefore, in them, the category of relation itself is dissolved (geht das Verhältniss selbst zu Grunde) and a new and higher principle of unity must emerge, that of Substance (Substanz) or the Actual (Wirkliche) which is the absolute unity of immediate and reflex existence.[100]

If this is the case, then it is clear that with the relation of Inner and Outer we have reached the limit of the category. Beyond this there is no longer relation but something higher still in the hierarchy of being. The genus of relation is, therefore, exhaustively divided into the three stated forms.

These three forms all contain the generic *ratio* of relation—that it is *in* or *of* Appearance—and they all have specifying differentiations within this genus. This result, from the text just cited,[101] enables us to answer provisionally a difficulty which we encountered earlier.[102] It is the one which arose because of Hegel's use of the terms "relation", "essential relation", "quantitative relation" and "absolute relation".[103] He states that "quantitative relation" occurs in the realm of Being (Seyn) before that of Essence (Wesen) and that "absolute relation" occurs in the realm of Essence but after Essential Relation.[104] Why should he speak in this way and then, at other times in a quite opposite

---
[97] *Ibidem*.
[98] *Logik* I, Cl. 4, p. 641.
[99] *Ibidem*.
[100] *Ibidem*.
[101] *Ibidem*.
[102] Text, p. 5 ff.
[103] *Ibidem*.
[104] *Ibidem*.

way, affirm that "essential relation" is identical with "relation" as such, without qualification?

The text just quoted gives a hint of an answer. It states that with Inner and Outer, relation itself is dissolved (geht zu Grunde)[105] and is then replaced by the higher categories of Substance, Causality and Mutual Interaction.[106] Now such a dissolution in the Heglian dialectic is not a destruction of the dissolved contents but their subsumption into a higher principle of unity, in which they are permitted to subsist.[107]. Thus the category of relation comes to subsist in that of Substance. Since this is the case, Substance itself may be denominated "relation". For it is all that relation is and more. Hegel, for this reason, calls it "absolute relation".[108]

Thus, if he speaks of *mere* relation or of *bare* relation, then "essential relation" and "relation as such" are completely identical for him, and relation itself is dissolved (geht zu Grunde) beyond that of Inner and Outer. But if he speaks of that which is *not mere* relation, but this and still more, then beyond "essential relation" there is also "absolute relation" and in this case "essential relation" is not identical with "relation as such".

A similar distinction provides an answer also to the problem of "quantitative relation" or "ratio". Just as "absolute relation" is *beyond* essential relation and thus exceeds it in perfection and, to this extent, is distinct from it, so "quantitative relation" is *before* essential relation and thus falls off from it in perfection, being thereby distinct from it. "Absolute relation" has a greater richness of being; quantitative relation has a lesser richness of being. Mere or bare relation ("essential relation") is in between.

These terminological clarifications provide, then, a certain understanding of Hegel's notion of relation. But they are far completely elucidating it, since they still leave the most important immediate point obscure. They yield no adequate grasp of what Appearance is, the category which defines relation and establishes its generic *ratio*. Until this is achieved, the result remains at best only mildly informative. The next chapter will attempt to remedy this situation.

---

[105]*Logik* I, Gl. 4, p. 641.
[106]*Ibidem*.
[107]*Phänomenologie des Geistes*, Gl. 2, p. 94; *Encyclopädie*, Gl. 8, p. 229.
[108]*Logik* I, Gl. 4, p. 641.

CHAPTER II

THE NATURE OF APPEARANCE

The nature of Appearance, as presented in the *Logic* and the *Phenomenology of Mind*, is identically the same. But in the latter it is treated of in so far as it is relative to the knowing subject (i.e. in so far as it appears in his consciousness); and in the former, in so far as it structured in itself, independently of its emergence in actual consciousness. This latter treatment is the more fundamental but it is not so clearly intelligible as the former which relates the thought of Hegel to the broad current of the history of philosophy.

A. THE NATURE OF APPEARANCE IN THE PHENOMENOLOGY OF MIND

The discussion of Appearance in the Phenomenology is prefaced by a description of sense knowledge and its objects. Sense knowledge, Hegel tells us, *seems* to be the richest knowledge and even to be unlimited in its variety.[1] It also seems to be the truest, most authentic and most certain.[2] Yet, if we reflect upon it, wihout thereby changing anything in it or in any way adding to it, we find that this is merely appearance.[3] In truth, sense knowledge is not the richest but rather the poorest, for it asserts of its object that it *is*, i.e. it qualifies the object with *being* and bare being alone.[4] It does not introduce relations which constitute the true richness of the known, nor is its object one which of itself postulates them.[5] Thus it is itself an im-

---

[1] *Phänomenologie des Geistes*, Gl. 2, p. 81. "The concrete content (Der konrete Inhalt) of sense certainty (der sinnlichen Gewissheit) makes it appear to e the richest knowledge (die reichalste Erkenntniss) and even a knowledge of finite richness (von unendlichem Reichthum) . . ."
[2] *Ibidem*.
[3] *Ibidem*.
[4] *Ib:dem*. "But this certainty (Diese Gewissheit) is really the most abstract (die abstrakteste) and the poorest (ärmste) truth (Wahrheit)."
[5] *Ibidem*, p. 82.

mediate and pure relation (unmittelbar reine Beziehung).[6] In sense consciousness there is only this: that the individual (der Einzelne) knows only the pure This (reines Dieses) or the Individual Thing (das Einzelne).[7]

This being so it is obvious that sense knowledge gives us a first distinction between appearance and truth. This is given in the differentiation between what seems to be true of the objects of sense (they seem to be the richest objects of knowledge and the most certain) and what is actually or in fact true of them (they are not the richest objects of knowledge but the poorest). By this distinction we are able to separate the immediate aspect of the object of sense from the mediate and more profound which lies beyond appearance and which is known only to reflection.[8] The immediate aspect of the object makes it appear as rich and certain; the object, as it is in itself, and therefore in *truth*, is bare and impoverished Being.

From this we may conclude that in order for the objects of sense to *appear* to sense, they must be qualified by *mere being*, which is to say that they must be constituted of this latter. This is a necessary but not a sufficient condition. Further investigation shows that more is required in order that sense objects *appear*.[9] A more searching consideration reveals that the object is presented to us (or appears to us) not merely as this sense certainty, but as an *example* of indefinitely many others.[10] This means that Appearance is essentially constituted by the relationship of example to model. The first manifestation of this is found in the fact that sense knowledge always involves the division of pure Beingness into "Thises", i.e. into the *this* which is the object, and the *this* which is the subject knowing.[1] The object of the knowledge cannot therefore appear except under this division. Thus, the latter constitutes its Appearance. To appear involves for it, as an essential presupposition, the separation of pure

---

[6] *Ibidem*.
[7] *Ibidem*.
[8] *Ibidem*.
[9] *Ibidem*, pp. 82, 83.
[10] *Ibidem*, p. 82. "An actual sense certainty is not only this pure immediac (diese reine Unmittelbarkeit), but also an example (ein Beispiel) of the same."
[11] *Ibidem*, p. 82. "From the innumerable distinctions which thus arise, v may separate out as the chief one (die Hauptverschiedenheit) . . . that of t two *thises* . . . the I and the object."

and mere Being into the "thisness" of subject knowing and of object known.[12]

But does this mean that the truly essential element in sense certainty, or in the object as it presents itself in the latter, is the object itself? Is this the essential factor of sense knowledge and is the knowing of it only a superadded accidental feature? This *seems* to be the case, at first glance, but a further look reveals that it is not.[13]

For sense certainty involves the correlation of two "Thises". Its object and its knowing subject have in common the fact of being "This."[14] But if we ask: What is the "This" in either—or: What is "Thisness" in itself?—then we must admit that it is the fact of being *here* and *now*.[15] But both *hereness* and *nowness* are universals, not singulars—contrary to what at first appears likely.[16] And therefore what constitutes the essential reality of sense certainty is universal, not singular.

Hegel attempts to corroborate this paradoxical conclusion by his famous example of "writing down the truth of the Here and Now." The truth of the Now, written down, is for example: The Now is night-time. This is not in any way affected by its being written down. Therefore, let it be written on a piece of paper and put away in a drawer. Several hours later let it be taken out again. At this later time, what is written on the paper is no longer true. For the Now has become day, which *is not night*. And thus the Now *is* in some way both day and night. Therefore it is a union of oppositions—of position and negation. Or, in other words, it is a Universal.[17]

But we have already seen that the Now together with the Here for which the same analysis can be made, so as to show that it too is a union of negation and position and therefore a Universal) constitutes the truth of sense certainty. Therefore the truth of sense certainty is the universal and not the singular.[18]

---

[12]*Ibidem.*
[13]*Ibidem,* p. 83.
[14]*Ibidem.*
[15]*Ibidem.*
[16]*Ibidem.*
[17]*Ibidem,* p. 84.
[18]*Ibidem,* p. 84. "The universal (das Allgemeine) is therefore in fact the truth sense certainty (das Wahre der sinnlichen Gewissheit)."

With regard to Appearance, this reveals to us something more of its structure. It is no longer reducible to bare Being as to its sufficient ultimate cause, but also to the universal, which, in fact, is Being also, although taken as abstracted and generalized. This is the ultimate cause of Appearance and the object is able to appear only by reason of this—the Universal to which it has the relation of example to model. [19]

But if this is true then it inverts the relationship between sense knowledge and sense object which Appearance seems to establish at the beginning. For it no longer allows us to hold that the essential reality lies in the object of sense knowledge; rather it forces us to posit the latter in the act of knowing itself.[20] For since, by this reasoning, the *Here* and *Now* are constitutive of the essential truth of sense certainty, and since they are essentially relative to the knowing of the object by the subject, this latter action now proves to be the essential truth of sensible appearance.[21] Thus, the object, of itself, is individual. It is universal only through the fact that it is contained in the *Here* and *Now* which pertains to the act of knowing. But Universality is the essential truth and reality of sense knowledge. Therefore the essential truth and reality of sense knowledge lies in the action of knowing itself. A sensible object is "true" because it is my object, i.e., because I *mean* it.[22]

Thus at this point in the *Phenomenology of Mind* appearance reveals itself as no simple relation of truth but a complex one, constituted of Being and knowledge. Hegel now tries to show that we are still far from its final cause and explanation.

This, he thinks, becomes evident if we reason to it from our acceptance of the truth of sense knowledge as universal. For this belief forces us to admit that truth is found in universal properties. But, if this is true, then it jeopardizes the distinctions of things. For many things are one in their properties. And therefore if we

---

[19]*Ibidem*, p. 84. Hegel shows how this fact is brought out by language which cannot "say" the strictly individual thing, but, being "truer" (wahrhafter) only the universal. Therefore we are able to *mean* (meinen) the strictly sensible being, but we cannot say it (sagen).
[20]*Ibidem*, p. 85. "The object, which was supposed to be the essential element (das Wesentliche) in sense certainty, has now become the non-essential (das Unwesentliche)."
[21]*Ibidem*.
[22]*Ibidem*, p. 85. "Truth is in the object in so far as it is *my* object."

stress these latter, we fuse the many into one. On the other hand, if we try to maintain their distinctness, we tend to suppress the oneness of their properties.[23]

This difficulty is, for Hegel, in essence the ancient one of the universals. And thus he brings this latter into the context of the *Phenomenology of Mind*, conceiving of it as a problem which merges with that of the constitution of things as they appear in knowledge, i.e. with the constitution of Appearance itself.

The truth of sense knowledge is therefore essentially its *universality*. But this means that such knowledge is both distinct and one. For its universality is that which is found in its many singulars, and its singularity is that which is contained within its universality.[24] And it makes an object appear by subsuming it as a singular under a universal form.

But, if this be so, it creates a new problem for us. For if, because of this, we stress the universality of sense truth, we seem forced to depreciate the singularity of sense objects. But if, on the other hand, we accentuate the singular, we seem forced to downgrade the universal.[25]

This difficulty Hegel then attempts to show may be resolved in three ways (by which contention he implies that there are only three distinct approaches theoretically possible and therefore historically achievable). The first way is to suppose that the apparent distinctions of the properties of sense objects are not distinction in reality but only in knowing.[26] From this it follows that things in themselves do not have such distinct properties but only in our knowledge of them.[27] Thus their real unity or universality is preserved, since they do not contain in themselves the dividing multiplicity of accidental characteristics. This is found only in the knowledge of them.[28] It is clear that, if this is true, the *appearance* of the thing known, or that which pertains to it *as appearing*, is reducible

---

[23]*Ibidem*, p. 93. "Since the principle of the object as universal is universality itself, this must express itself, and it does this, manifesting itself as a thing having many properties (das Ding von vielen Eigenschaften)."
[24]*Ibidem*, pp. 101, 102.
[25]*Ibidem*, p. 103.
[26]*Ibidem*, p. 105.
[27]*Ibidem*, p. 106.
[28]*Ibidem*.

to the knowing subject and not to an objective cause. Appearance, then, is constituted by knowledge itself and not by any objective factors.

A second way to resolve the problem is to suppose that the multiplicity of aspects is real, and that the unity of the object is the product of the mind. Hegel calls this resolution the theory of the "congeries", obviously having Locke in mind. According to it the real world is a discrete quantity without any principle of unity. When this world enters the mind or, in other words, when it appears to the latter, it does so only because in the act of being perceived its disparate elements are grouped into some sort of mental wholes or unity.[29] Thus its unity is reducible to the action of the mind and is therefore not an ontological phenomenon or problem, but a mental one.[30]

Hegel criticizes this solution, as well as the first one, by contending that they do not really deal with the problem at all, for they do not attempt to reconcile universality with singularity. This reconciliation must take place in the objective or in the subjective field, and of course, it may take place in both. If it occurs in the objective field it must reconcile universal and singular thingness; if, in the subjective field, universal and singular knowledge. Neither effect is achieved by the two theories just considered, for they both posit unity in one field and multiplicity in the other. Thus both fail to resolve the problem.

The recognition that this is so leads the mind to make still another attempt at a solution by supposing that one must distinguish the essential and unchanging properties of things from their non-essential and changing properties.[31] If this distinction is made, then it possible to assert that sensible objects are one according to the non-essential properties, but distinct, according to their essential one In this way they are both universal (related to other things) and singular (isolated in themselves).[32] Hegel considers this solution as untenable. For, he reasons, it is necessary that some relation be admitted between the unchanging essence of the thing and its chang

---

[29] Findlay, *Hegel*, pp. 91, 92.
[30] *Ibidem*.
[31] *Ibidem*.
[32] *Ibidem*.

able non-essential properties and it is necessary also to admit some sort of connection between the supposed multiple essentialities. And both of these necessary admissions render the position absurd.[33]

Thus the *congeries* theory, in trying to reduce the structure of Appearance to the action of the mind by attributing to the latter the unity of the thing known, identifies Appearance with "unification of a multiplicity by the mind." But that such could in fact be the case is impossible or, at the very least, irrelevant since the theory either cannot or does not reduce the conflict which Appearance presents since it does not reconcile the universality and singularity of the latter, either objectively or subjectively.[34]

The solution based upon the distinction of essential and non-essential properties, on the other hand, does make an attempt to do this from the side of the object, but it fails to achieve its goal. For, in asserting that there is an unchangeable core of essential properties together with a changeable periphery of non-essential ones, it overlooks the fact that the former and the latter must somehow be connected (otherwise the changing properties cannot be held to pertain to the essential core) and that this connection destroys the isolation which the theory attempts to achieve.[35] Thus it too is no acceptable solution of the problem of Appearance.

With this third endeavor, the effort to solve the problem comes to a temporary halt leaving the puzzling nature of Appearance unexplained. Moreover, it cannot be taken up again and pushed further if the factors involved in the three preceding theories are the only ones admitted.[36] Further progress is possible only if, to sensible properties of connected things in a sensible world, there is added the factor of a non-sensible world.[37]

The addition of this new element, Hegel feels, forces us to admit a two-world explanation. One of these is that of sensible

---

[33]*Ibidem.*
[34]*Ibidem.*
[35]*Ibidem*, p. 92. "The changing aspects must have *some* root in its unchanging essence, and this unchanging essence must itself be compared, and therefore connected, with external things. And, of course, the connection is a *relation*, and, as such, a dependency. And thus the attempt to explain the situation by supposing an unrelated essence collapses."
[36]*Ibidem*, p. 92.
[37]*Ibidem*, p. 92. "The diversity of aspects or properties of the Thing is held to belong to the world of sensory appearance, but to have a backing in a reality realities which lie behind the scenes at some *deeper* or *inner* level."

things attainable in sense knowledge, i.e., in observation. The other is that of non-sensible things which are therefore not observable.[38] This latter world brings it about that the diverse and multiple properties of sensible things in truth belong to them, but not in so far as they are sensible—rather only in so far as they are unobservable underlying principle.[39] This notion, for Hegel, projects the mind into the realm of Scientific Understanding.[40]

In this new realm, he affirms, Appearance is reduced to an underlying unobservable principle as to its objective cause.[41] This is the source of its structure. It is this which constitutes it and thus makes it objective.[42] So Appearance is explained in the *Phenomenology of Mind* and relation is associated with it as its constitutive principle.

In this work Appearance is posited as caused by its relation to an objective principle. If this is true, it cannot exist unless the relation too exists as well as the unobserved principle in which the relation terminates. Thus Appearance is both relational and objectively grounded.[43]

The grounding is not a simple one but the account given of it in the *Phenomenology of Mind* is less complex than that given in the greater *Logic*. In the latter work, it is said to arise from three distinct relational movements. In the *Phenomenology of Mind*, only one of these is considered—that of Force and its Manifestation. This, for the second work, constitutes *Appearance*. Appearance is the *manifestation* of an underlying non-observable principle which, in so far as it manifests, is Force. This being so Appearance is not simply a relation to sense, nor a unity established in a sensible diversity by the action of sensation, nor is it anything else which can adequately be explained by factors restricted to the sensible and observable world. Rather, it is something which finds an adequate explanation only in its relation to an underlying principle, as to a Force of which it is the Manifestation.[44] This, for Hegel, in the *Phenomenology*, is its nature. The *Logic*, and the other more specialized treatises, ad

---

[38]*Ibidem.*
[39]*Ibidem*, p. 92; *Phänomenologie das Geistes*, Gl. 2, p. 107.
[40]*Ibidem.*
[41]*Ibidem.*
[42]*Ibidem.*
[43]*Ibidem.*
[44]*Phänomenologie des Geistes*, Gl. 2, p. 113.

that the category of relation is therefore correlative to that of Appearance and that relation thus occurs at that point in the structure of reality where Being becomes *immediately apparent*.

The remainder of the *Phenomenology*, in which Hegel shows how the apparent is not an absolute term but only a middle stage, does not concern us except to the extent that it locates the phenomenal as a medium between bare being and Absolute Self-consciousness, and thus shows that the division between the underlying reality and its manifestation or between the apparent thing and the mind to which it appears, is resolved in the higher unity of the Notion, or the Idea.[45] From this it follows that, for Hegel, relation is itself resolved in a higher non-relational content. This latter is therefore its ultimate explanation through which alone it can be adequately understood. But we must now return to our immediate problem—the nature of Appearance itself—and this time as it is presented in the *Logic*.

B. The Nature of Appearance in the Logic

In the *Logic*, Hegel exposes in considerable detail the stages through which object and subject must pass to arrive at Absolute Knowledge in which total unity is had. In doing this he is forced to decide first of all what he will take as the beginning of the process. He considers this problem in an interesting preface of Book One of the section on Being, where he first discusses various beginnings which have been proposed by others and then decides on his own— that the true beginning is Indeterminate Being.[46] Indeterminate Being, he postulates, or Being in itself without further determination, must be the start of philosophical thought.[47] From this he then builds step by step to the structure of Appearance.

It is interesting to note of this choice that it is the same which St. Thomas makes for rational thought. In other words, what Aquinas takes as first in the order of rational knowledge, Hegel takes as first in the order of reality.[48] And what, for St. Thomas, is the root

---

[45] *Ibidem*, p. 335.
[46] *Logik* I, Gl. 4, p. 77 ff. "It lies in the nature of the beginning itself (in der Natur des Anfangs selbst) that it should be being (Seyn) and nothing else und sonst Nichts)."
[47] *Ibidem*.
[48] Aquinas, *Summa Theologiae*, I, II, q. 55, art. 4, ad 2 "Ad primum ergo dicendum quod id quod primo cadit in intellectu, est ens: unde unicuique apprehenso a nobis attribuimus quod sit ens."

of all conceptualization—the abstract ratio of being—is for Hegel a constitutive principle of reality.[49] And thus what Aquinas considers properties of things in so far as they are thought by reason—abstraction, negation and so forth—Hegel considers as ontological structuring causes.[50]

His beginning, then, is in pure being. This is an indeterminate immediacy for if it had determination it would not be immediate and a cause, but mediated and caused.[51] And its indeterminacy, which is thus essential to it, is such that it is totally vacuous and lacks any principle of distinction. For this reason no determined content can be intuited in it. It is a pure nothingness.[52]

Having satisfied himself that this is so Hegel then goes on to consider a problem which arises from it: that Being is, therefore, in one sense, opposed to Nothing, and, in another sense, identified with it. He argues that, if this is true, Being cannot exist except in a higher principle which sustains its oppositions. This principle he identifies as that of Becoming.[53]

Becoming is thus the reconciliation of Being and Nothing.[54] But this means that it contains within itself indeterminateness and determinateness, the first, as Being, and the second, as Nothing. For Nothing limits or determines the indeterminateness of Being, and in doing this, qualifies the latter.[55] For this reason, Becoming manifests itself as *Determinate Being*.[56] In fact, Determinate Being issues from it.[57]

Since this is so, it follows that Appearance too is rooted in Being, as we have already seen in the *Phenomenology of Mind*.[58] But that work does not give, as does the *Logic,* the complete structure of this grounding by which Being advances to appearance. The *Phenomenology* starts with Appearance and seeks subsequently to discover the suppositions behind it. This treatment is therefore the inverse

---

[49]*Logik* I, Gl. 4, pp. 69 ff.
[50]*Ibidem*, p. 122.
[51]*Phänomenologie des Geistes,* Gl. 2, p. 81; *Logik* I, Gl. 4, p. 87.
[52]*Logik* I, Gl. 4, p. 88.
[53]*Ibidem*, p. 89 ff.
[54]*Ibidem.*
[55]*Ibidem.*
[56]*Ibidem,* p. 89.
[57]*Ibidem,* p. 119.
[58]Text, p. 34.

THE NATURE OF APPEARANCE 29

of that of the *Logic,* which starts from the suppositions and works forward from these to the constitutive principles of Appearance.

Hegel shows how this occurs first of all by the qualification or determination of Being.[59] The result of this is a combination of Determinable Being and Determining Limit. But this latter may be added indefinitely to the former, since Being has a capacity for indefinite determination, which Hegel conceives to be its "false infinity". This is the "false infinity" of qualified being, or of the category of Quality. The true infinity of this category, on the other hand, is that higher principle of unity which assumes into itself all of the negations and positions of the false, and thereby conserves them.[60] It is the being-for-self (Fürsichseyn), which gives rise to Quantity and thus to the second of the categories within the sphere of Being.[61]

Hegel then discusses the intricate structure of this category showing how, at the end, it too leads to the still higher category—that of Measure.[62] This must occur, he holds, because it is necessary that the diversity of Quality and Quantity should be reconciled in some higher principle, which is at once quality and quantity. And this is Measure.[63] But it, too, evolves, emerging, at its apex, into the broad realm of *Essence,* or *Wesen.*

Thus Essence is not the same thing as Being. This is evident from the fact that it is posterior to the latter and developed from it by a tissue of relations, as Hegel asserts.[64]

Compared with this, scholastic thought is found to be quite different. What Hegelian doctrine posits as real relations structuring essence on the foundation of Being, scholastic doctrine posits as relations of reason. This is certainly most clear in the Hegelian conception of the category of Quality (Determined Being), which is not the scholastic category of real quality, but its logical category of "predicability."[65] It is true that this latter, even in scholastic tradition, is sometimes conceived of as a sort of qualification, as in the

[59] *Logik* I, Gl. 4, p. 139 ff.
[60] *Ibidem*, p. 147 and p. 157 ff.
[61] *Ibidem*, p. 183.
[62] *Ibidem*, p. 405.
[63] *Ibidem.*
[64] *Ibidem*, p. 481. "Die Wahrheit des Seyns ist das Wesen."
[65] Aristotle, *Categories* V, 3 b 20 ff. where *second substance* is compared to a quality.

much quoted phrase from Aristotle.[66] But this is always understood in an analogous sense. A predicate is held to qualify a subject in a proposition in a different way from that in which a sensible form qualifies a material body.

But this category of Quality is not the only one which is strange, from a scholastic point of view. There is also that of Quantity, which is not the same in the conception of the two philosophical currents. For the scholastic, the quantity of Hegel is the quantity of a proposition or of a concept, i.e. of things thought as such. It is not the ontological quantity which individuates real things. This fact makes the scholastic mind conclude that Hegel is attempting to reduce the structure of reality to relations of reason. It is by these that he attempts to explain constituent principles of Appearance.

For he reduces Appearance to the need of Essence to manifest itself in order not to be a pure abstraction. This need is therefore a cause of Appearance whereby Essence gains Existence as a matter of fact.[67] But for Essence thus to manifest itself, it must first be *in itself*. Only then can it go outside of itself, since being first in itself is the condition for its emergence.[68] But it is impossible that it should be thus first in itself and then outside, while remaining the same identical thing, unless it be assumed into a higher principle of unity which can sustain this contradiction.[69] This is, in fact, what happens: Essence is so assumed into a higher reconciling principle, and it thereby becomes Actuality.[70] Now, it is the going outside of itself on the part of Essence that constitutes the category of Appearance. And thus it is by the relation of exteriorization (negation) and reconciliation (negation of negation) that Hegel, in the *Logic*, explains and defines this category.[71]

It is interesting to note that he posits, as a first stage in this exteriorization, the category of *Existence*.[72] This, for him, is the preparation of Essence for perfect exteriorization. Or, in other words,

[66] *Ibidem.*
[67] *Logik* I, Gl. 4, p. 592 ff. The subject is treated under the title of "The Emergence of the Thing into Existence" (Hervorgang der Sache in die Existenz
[68] *Ibidem*, p. 598.
[69] *Ibidem*, p. 662.
[70] *Ibidem.*
[71] *Ibidem*, p. 598.
[72] *Ibidem.*

Essence, immediately prepared for relation to itself as outside of itself, is, for Hegel, Existence or the Existing Thing.

Once Essence thus achieves Existence it then naturally passes over into a stricter exteriority, i.e. it naturally goes completely outside of itself.[73] And in this relation to itself, it is Phenomenal Being in the strict sense. Appearance is therefore completely exteriorized Essence.[74]

If this is true, it is obvious that it puts Essence into contradiction with itself. So Hegel reasons. For, he asserts, by this situation, Essence is made to exist and to appear.[75] But it is one, whereas its Appearance is multiple. This contradiction, he holds, is resolved in the relationship which is most fundamental here—that of Whole and Part.[76] And thus this relation constitutes Appearance.

Thus, until it is added, the apparent and the existing threaten to destroy each other because each is negative to the other. They can therefore only avoid this result by being assumed into a higher principle of unity. This occurs when they are received into the unity of the relation of Whole and Part which, by that fact, becomes the first higher principle of unity whereby the Existing and the Phenomenal, both grounded in Essence, are reconciled.[77]

But this reconciliation is not final. For the existing thing manifests itself dynamically, not statically. And for this mode of manifestation the relation of Whole and Part is insufficient. It must therefore be superseded by another—the relation of Force and Manifestation.[78] This new relation permits a dynamical manifestation in which the parts of the whole are not all present at once, but only successively. And again, since such a mode of being supposes an inner something which remains unchanged throughout the changing manifestations, it therefore gives rise to the relationship of Inner and Outer.[79] Finally, since, in this latter, the Inner can take the place of the Outer, they prove to be, in fact, one and the same thing, only relationally distin-

---

[73]*Ibidem*, p. 622.
[74]*Ibidem*.
[75]*Ibidem*.
[76]*Ibidem*, p. 641.
[77]*Ibidem*.
[78]*Ibidem*, p. 648.
[79]*Ibidem*, p. 655.

guished. Thus, in this one thing, the opposition of relation itself resolves into the unity of the absolute.[80]

And with this we have achieved our purpose. The meaning of Appearance for Hegel, as he presents this in the *Logic*, is clear. And from this we can now explain the various definitions of relation already considered in which Appearance is genus. In a general way, they mean that we must understand Hegelian relation as intimately bound up with existence and essence. Because of this, we cannot understand it without reference to them. But, on the other hand, we cannot understand them without reference to it. This presents us with a problem which we shall consider in the next chapter.

---

[80] *Ibidem*, p. 663.

CHAPTER III

THE BROADER NOTION OF RELATION IN HEGEL

The problem, to which the considerations of the preceding chapter have led us, is that of a broader notion of relation in Hegel. Stace recognizes that it is a valid one.[1] For he agrees that one might reasonably object to Hegel's location of the category within the realm of Appearance. One might well affirm that all through the category of Essence—and therefore long before the category of Appearance is reached—one is dealing with relation and correlation of various sorts.[2] In particular, the mutual dependence involved in reflection (the reflection of Essence into itself whereby it is Essence in itself) is nothing more or less than relation.[3] Nevertheless, Stace thinks, this is not of much importance. It is a purely terminological matter.[4] What Hegel calls "relation" is clearly and sharply defined by his explanation of it. That he should prefer to apply the name of "relation" to this content in particular is thus a matter of choice[5] and as long as this choice is understood by us, it does not create a difficulty.

But Stace is not fully convinced by this reasoning since he qualifies it by stating that the choice is perhaps "not a very appropriate one" or not a "happy one".[6] Why is it not appropriate? Clearly for the reason that the word is not so proportioned to this one sharply defined

---

[1] Stace, *The Philosophy of Hegel*, p. 203. "It might reasonably be objected that we have been dealing with categories of relation throughout the whole of the doctrine of essence . . ."
[2] *Ibidem:* ". . . and further that the mutual dependence involved in reflection is the same thing as correlation."
[3] *Ibidem.*
[4] *Ibidem.* "This is no doubt true, but it is a matter of mere terminology."
[5] *Ibidem.*
[6] *Ibidem:* "The selection may not be a very appropriate or happy one. But as long as we understand the sense in which he uses the words this does not matter."

content that it could be said to belong to it more than to others. This is not so supereminently relation that the word is most proper to it. And why is the application of the word an unhappy one? Obviously because the natural tendancy of anyone is to apply it in a more general way than Hegel does, that is to say, to understand it somewhat differently. This being the case the student of Hegel is forced continually to correct this tendency in order not to falsify the philosopher's thought.

Now this difficulty, which Stace thus points out and then sets aside, is obviously important. Moreover it exists for relation alone of all the categories whose structure Hegel analyzes and exposes. All of the other categories occupy precisely determined positions. Relation alone is ambiguous.

So, for example, no one could confuse the Hegelian category of Quantity with that of Quality. And it is clear to all which of these has precedence and how the two are ordered one to the other. But this is not the case for the category of relation. It is not at all clear that this occupies one determined position alone. And this forces Hegel at times to qualify his affirmations about it in order to avoid inconsistency.[7]

An example of this is given at the beginning of the *Logic*, where he is forced to distinguish general relation from relation in *measure*:

> "Measure is a relation, though not Relation in general, but a definite relation—that of Quantity to Quality."[8]

Another example is found in the definition already cited:

> Relation (Verhältniss) is a reference (Beziehung) of two sides one to the other . . .[9]

In translating this, it is difficult not to say:

> "Relation is a relation . . ."

For both "Verhältniss" and "Beziehung" signify a common relational nature. Hegel has, therefore, to force their sense in order to distinguish them. He has to stress the aspect of "two sides" as differentiating "Verhältniss".[10] But of course this does not distinguish the reflection of

---

[7]*Logik* I, Gl. 4, p. 86.
[8]*Ibidem.*
[9]Footnote no. 10, p. 3.
[10]*Logik* I, Gl. 4, 640 ff.

Essence into itself (which also has two sides) from "Verhältniss", as Stace points out.[11]

With With respect to the category of Measure, which Hegel explicitly calls "relation", it is clear that its relationality could not be identical with that which constitues Appearance. Measure is not measure, for Hegel, through Whole and Part, Force and its Manifestation, or Inner and Outer. These cannot be applied to it. This being the case it must be what it is by the application of some other sort of relation to it, as Hegel explicitly affirms.[12] This is reasonable enough. But still it creates the supicion that we are here dealing in fact with a general *ratio* of relation and distinct species. If this is the case, it would not appear that Hegel is justified in applying the generic name to the specific manifestation found in the category of Appearance.

This conviction is further strengthened by the practice of the Hegelian commentators. For they, in discussing relation, view it not as the constituting principle of Appearance alone, but of the entire structure of Being and Thought.

This is clearly what Bradley means when he tells us that "qualities without relations are nothing".[13] For by this expression he puts relation into the context of quality, that is to say, into the category of Determined Being, prior to that of Appearance. It is this category which embodies the essence of the relational for him. And because it does, he can therefore assert that "relation supposes quality and quality relation".[14] And again, for the same reason, he can ask if qualities without relation have any meaning and answer that they do not[15]. Thus it is perfectly clear that for him relation is not the restricted reference of the category of Appearance but the general one of the category of Quality co-extensive with predication.[16]

These remarks together with those already made in the second chapter should be sufficient to show that there is a problem in Hegel as to the meaning of relation. It has, in fact, many meanings. And before we can judge the Hegelian doctrine on it, we must first establish these latter. We will attempt to do this by developing in more detail those

---

[11] Stace, *The Philosophy of Hegel*, p. 203.
[12] *Logik* I, Gl. 4, p. 476 ff.
[13] Bradley, *Appearance and Reality*, p. 585.
[14] *Ibidem*, p. 25.
[15] *Ibidem*, p. 29.
[16] Bradley, *Essays on Truth and Reality*, p. 228; *Appearance and Reality*, p. 20; Hegel, *Encyclopedia*, Gl. 8, p. 204.

areas of the Hegelian analysis where some particular sort of relation seems to be employed. When this has been done it will then be possible for us to order and compare the results.

A. The Presence of a Broader Notion of Relation in Hegel.

1. In the Category of Quality: Becoming

The first place where we notice the use of a particular relation is in the beginning of the *Logic*. There Hegel tells us that pure indetermined being is the absolute principle of science.[17] But, he goes on to show, it is not the end. For it essentially points beyond itself to Nonbeing or *Nothing*. It *is not* Nothing.[18] This negativity is a relation (Beziehung) which cannot be separated from its nature. Thus by nature it is what it is through *relation*.[19]

Having established this point Hegel then tries to show that a consequence is the admission that Being and Non-being are identical. He argues to this in two ways: first, by analyzing the contents of both and thus showing that ultimately there is no difference between them; secondly, by analyzing the nature of the relations which constitute both.

In the first argument he reasons that if we consider the content of Being we see that it is absolutely empty. For it contains no determination and therefore none can be intuited in it. In this it is in no way different from Nonbeing, and thus the two, in the final analysis, are one and the same thing.[20]

In the second argument he points out that if we admit that Being is all that it is by its relation to Nonbeing, then we must go further and admit also that this relation is of its essence. The same may be asserted of Nonbeing. Its relation to being too is its essence. Therefore Nonbeing is contained in Being and Being in Nonbeing, and they are one and the same.[21]

The relation, which structures Being in both of these arguments, is what the scholastic would call one of reason, linking together things

---

[17]*Logik* I, p. 87.
[18]*Ibidem*, p. 88.
[19]*Ibidem*.
[20]*Ibidem*.
[21]*Encyclopädie*, Gl. 8, p. 207.

which are disparate in thought alone—being and the *ens rationis*, nonbeing. Hegel attributes to it a property which is attributed by the scholastics to the so-called *transcendental relation*—that of being embedded in a nature rather than added to it. This property does not lead the Thomist to identify its terms in reality. But it does lead Hegel to do so for reasons which we will consider further on.[22] For the moment let us note only that because he conceives of Being as essentially relative to Nonbeing, Hegel can then enrich his notion of it with the idea of its "going outside of itself". This is simply another way of conceiving its relativity to Nonbeing. For it is itself both the beginning and the term of this relativity. But in so far as it is the term, it is opposed to itself. And this is a sort of "going outside of itself".[23] On the other hand, since it is the beginning too, it is therefore "in itself" and this being "in itself" is the basis which permits it thereafter to "go outside of itself".[24] The relational complexity of this situation reaches its climax in the Hegelian conception that Being is in itself, ultimately, through being outside of itself, and therefore that the latter permits *reflection*.[25] Thus, in the final analysis, Being is relational to Nonbeing, and Nonbeing is relational to Being, having existence through the particular relation of "exclusion from being".[26]

This analysis, though still incomplete, is nevertheless sufficient to show that at the very beginning of science, relation has a fundamental structuring role for Hegel. Moreover it shows that the relation which has this role is not any relation whatsoever, nor the specific relations which pertain to the category of Appearance—Whole and Part, and so forth—but the relations of "position" and "negation" and "identification", which Hegel denominates "Beziehungen".[27] He conceives of these movements of the one fundamental ratio of "Beziehung" (reference).[28] Thus he holds that "relation" (Beziehung), as divided into these two movements, is the fundamental structuring principle of thought and reality.

But these are not its only movements. Hegel now introduces another by remarking, first of all, that the situation which he has attributed

---

[22]Cf. Chapter Four, sec. C.
[23]*Logik* I, p. 119 and p. 183, Gl. 4.
[24]*Logik* I, p. 84, Gl. 4.
[25]*Ibidem*.
[26]*Ibidem*, p. 88.
[27]*Logik* I, p. 640, Gl. 4.
[28]*Ibidem*.

to Being and Nonbeing could not possibly be ultimate, since it is self-negating and therefore self-destroying if unsupported.[29] For by it Being is both in itself and outside of itself; harmonious with and identical to itself, and at the same time in intrinsic conflict. It must therefore simply cease to be unless some way can be found to prevent this.

This problem is similar to that which is posed by scholastic transcendental relations. These are totally correlative one to the other and thus depend upon one another in order to be, as, for example, potency depends upon act and act upon potency. For potency is what it is by reference to its act and its act is what it is by a reverse reference to potency. Thus, in order for potency to be, act must first be. At the same time, act cannot be unless it is received by potency, and is therefore consequent upon it. Because of this both exclude each another from being, unless sustained by a third relation which is, in the final analysis, to an extrinsic simple cause.

From a formal point of view Hegel's argument is similar. For *Being* and *Nothing*, as he conceives of them, stand one to the other in somewhat the same relationship as act and potency. They are likewise totally correlative such that one cannot exist without the other. And at the same time, left to themselves, they exclude one another from being. Hegel concludes from this that unless they are reconciled in some higher principle of unity, they cannot be maintained. But, he holds, they are in fact maintained, since they do not, in fact, destroy each other. From this he concludes that a higher sustaining principle must exist.

Thus, just as the scholastic extrinsic simple cause sustains the potency-act compound, so this Hegelian principle of unification sustains the "compound" of negation and position. And just as the former involves in itself none of the limitations of the composed thing which it sustains, so the Hegelian principle of unification is a "lifting" of contradiction.

There are, of course, radical differences in the two positions. Scholastic doctrine does not identify the extrinsic cause with the compounded thing which it sustains, but Hegel does. His principle is identical with the self-contradictory content which its supports. It is a cause which is immanent in its effect. And it causes the effect by "emerging"

[29]*Logik* I, Gl. 4, p. 88.
[30]*Ibidem*, pp. 88 ff.

since it may be said to "emerge" by being in itself, then, outside of itself, and finally in itself again by a sort of return or reflection. Hegel calls this last movement that of "being by itself" (bei sich seyn). And in the context of his dialectic this signifies that it is an immanent process of emergent reflection into self.

But whatever may be the ontological difference between the two doctrines, their formal or logical similarity is so striking as to argue for a common source. For the scholastic teaching, this source is the Platonic and Aristotelian metaphysical doctrine of participation with its postulation of Nous and Anima as causes of intelligible and animated things. For Hegel, as it is not at all difficult to establish from his writings, the source is the same. This is strikingly confirmed in the last paragraph of his *Encyclopedia of the Philosophical Sciences* which is a citation in the Greek of Aristotle's famous passage on the Nous.

Now if this identity of source is grounded, then it justifies the use of the traditional doctrine as a key to interpret the Hegelian dialectic. This means that the third relation in the Hegelian triad—that of reconciliation (Aufgehobenheit)—may be conceived of as similar to the traditional relation between participating things and that from which they participate. So, in the present case, the relation of *being* and *nonbeing* to their principle of conservation may be understood as similar to that which holds between act and potency (in a composed thing) with respect to their ultimately simple external cause. The principle of reconciliation in Hegel resembles the simple external cause of the Neoplatonic tradition in the property of simplicity too. For it is one whereas the things which it units are many and opposed. It therefore contains in a simple way what they have by composition.

Moreover like the separated forms of the Neo-platonic tradition Hegel's principles of higher unification are many and hierarchically ordered. It is, in fact, this diversity in order which constitutes the structure of reality. And in that structure the immediate principle of of unification following upon the opposition of Being and Nonbeing is that of *Becoming*.[31]

It follows from this that the Hegelian doctrine of Becoming shows the latter to be essentially a consequence of relation and, in particular, one similar to that which holds between Nous and intelligible things or between Anima and animated things in the Neoplatonic tradition.

[31] *Ibidem*.

For our purposes this suffices to show the presence of relation in the Hegelian structure of being as well as its fundamental importance there. It also shows that this relation is *not* the one defined by the "category of relation". Thus we are forced to recognize a fundamental division within the *ratio* of relation. It is that which is found in the realm of Essence and constitutes the structure of Appearance. It is also that which is found in the realm of Being and constitutes its structure too. This second relation is obviously the more fundamental.

The peculiar interpretation of Becoming as the reconciliation of Being and Nonbeing is objected against by many philosophers. Certainly it seems to put the most concrete element of experience in immediate contact with the most abstract (pure being and pure nothing). A more likely position for Becoming would seem to be the category of Appearance. For Becoming seems to be the aspect which predominates in the phenomenal.

This is, perhaps valid enough. But there are other even more important objections, such as the scholastic one against the interpretation of real being in terms of purely rational relations. The Thomist cannot admit that negation and affirmation are, as such, ontological principles. And he cannot therefore admit that they constitute the realty of becoming. However our purpose now is not to consider the validity of the Hegelian construction of being, but only its nature. And with respect to this purpose the situation is clear. Relation is the prime structuring principle of Becoming, and thus serves to *constitute* Becoming *essentially*. Becoming is no more than a principle of unity, that is to say a relationship of reconciliation to the negation and position which constitute Being and Nonbeing.

Therefore relation is present in the structure of Becoming and Being under three forms:

1. position
2. negation
3. reconciliation (negation of negation)

Moreover none of these forms is the same as that defined in the category of relation. They have, it is true, the same common *ratio* of reference (Beziehung) but they have this ratio in a more generic way, since they can be applied immediately to Being, whereas the category of relation cannot. Thus there is a form of relation in the realm of Being quite distinct from that found in the category of relation.

2. In the Category of Quality: Determined Being

If the reconciliation achieved by Becoming were final, it would rest in itself as a term. Hegel assures us that it does not do so. It is therefore not final but itself a beginning with respect to something higher and, for this reason, supposes new relations at play in the structure of reality or the prior relations employed with respect to new terms. It is this second position which Hegel chooses.

At least this appears to be the case, for the names which he employs to designate the new relations are the same as those for the realm of bcoming: position, negation and reconciliation. But the use to which he puts them is not so clearly the same. And this makes some of his commentators think that they are, in fact, different.[32] This difficulty can be set aside if we apply the doctrine of participation to their interpretation. For participation permits an indefinite variety of forms in a relationship which is analogically one.

At all events Hegel explains the process beyond Becoming in this way. Becoming, if closely considered, is seen itself to contain internal contradictions. But whatever is internally contradictory by that fact is inwardly constituted of "position" and "negation".[33] And whatever is so constituted if left to itself will destroy itself. To avoid this it must seek a higher principle of reconciliation. Thus Becoming seeks such a principle, that is to say it goes beyond itself into a unity by which it is sustained.[34]

Findlay, in commenting upon this reasoning, remarks that its derivation is obscure—the derivation, that is, of "determined being" from "becoming". This does not unduly disturb him, and he is satisfied with a vague interpretation of Hegel's meaning.[35] Hegel intends only to assert that there must be something hard and fast in the world beyond the fluidity of becoming. This may be so, in a certain sense, but it hardly seems adequate as a key to the structure of "determined being" and it is clearly this structure which most concerns Hegel.

This being the case it would seem to do more justice to his obvious intent if we were to conceive his description of the structure of Determinate Being as an extrapolation of the structure of Becoming. In do-

---

[32] Findlay, *Hegel*, pp. 72, 73, 74, 109; E. Coreth, *op. cit.*, p. 19; N. Hartmann, *Hegel und das Problem der Realdialektik*, Bl. f. dt. Phil. 9 (1935/36), p. 5.
[33] *Logik* I, Gl. 4, p. 119 ff.
[34] *Ibidem*.
[35] Findlay, *Hegel*, p. 158.

ing this we may understand Hegel as taking the triadic relational complexus already discovered to constitute the realm of Becoming, and applying it again to that of Determined Being with Becoming now not the term of the relation of reconciliation but rather the beginning. This understanding permits us to maintain reserve concerning the justification for this particular application of the dialectical triad, while at the same gaining insight into Hegel's thought.

But whether the application is justified or not is not so important here. What is of import is the fact that Hegel again exposes the structure of reality in terms of relations, and that he does so using the same relations which he has already used in the structuring of Becoming, that is to say such as do not pertain to the category of relation.

The category of Determined Being which thus emerges contains the same dialectical triad. For it is first in itself by a "position" which is therefore essentially correlative to a "negative". Then it is outside of itself by a negation which can be nothing other than its finitude or limitation.[36] Finally it returns into itself by negation of negation.

At this point in the *Logic* Hegel introduces the strange doctrine of "false" and "true" infinity.[37] This is worthy of close consideration for the fruitful insight which it affords into the nature of the relation of reconciliation. Hegel remarks that the limitations of determined being can be indefinite and that this is a sort of infinity, one, in fact, which seems the only genuine infinity to many. But, he notes, there is another infinity found in that principle which stands above all finite determinations, reconciling them in its unity and this is of a much higher order. It is the *true* infinity relative to which the other is *false*.[38]

The Thomist cannot help but be struck by this conception. For it is identical with that which he has of the *per se* as opposed to the *per participationem*.[39] For, according to his traditional doctrine, the *per se* is infinite in its own genus and is the cause of the indefinitely many finite participating things which depend upon this genus. So, for example, color per se, if it could be made to exist in separation from colored things, would be infinite. Infinity pertains to this state

---

[36]*Logík* I, Gl. 4, p. 121.
[37]*Ibidem*, pp. 157, 158; 302, 303, 305.
[38]*Ibidem*.
[39]Aquinas, *Summa Theologiae*, I, 96, art. 1, corp.

whereas finitude pertains to the state of the participating.[40] St. Thomas discusses this matter in some detail in his commentary on the Liber de Causis.[41] In this work he shows how the separated forms are, for the Platonists, so many infinities.[42] The potential infinity in the multiplication of participations does not equal this higher sort which is free of the contrarieties found in participating things.[43]

The similarity between this doctrine and the Hegelian one of "infinity" in the category of Determined Being is too close to be an accident. If this be true then it seems legitimate to conclude that what Hegel calls "true infinity" is that sort which is the general property of the reconciling principle with respect to the multiplicity which it reconciles, that is to say is the infinity of the *per se* in the traditional doctrine.

Thus in the Hegelian analysis as in the traditional one, infinity explains multiplicity and the "true infinity" is the cause of the "false". The order of these two is not the same in Hegel and in the tradition, but their formality is.

One obvious difference is the priority of the "false infinity" in Hegel. For him *true infinity* emerges from it as a cause. In the traditional doctrine the reverse is the case. There "true infinity" comes first and the world of participating things follows upon it.

At all events he does not think that with the positing of the "true infinity" the extrapolation of the triadic dialectic is at an end. For, as he tries to show, the principle itself becomes a point of departure for a higher movement. It posits itself as identical with itself; then it goes outside of itself through negation; and finally it returns into itself as reconciling both the position and the negation in a still higher principle of unity. In this way it gives rise first to *Unity* and *Plurality*, and then to *Repulsion* and *Attraction*.

Our primary interest in this exposition is again to establish by it the function of relation. For this purpose it will help us to consider the reasons which lead Hegel to the particular terms which he assigns, since these elucidate the "negativity" and the "reconciliation" which are the fundamental relations involved.

---

[40]*Ibidem*, I, 7, 1, corp.
[41]Aquinas, *In Librum De Causis Expositio*, Prop. XVI, no. 318 (ed. Para, p. 97).
[42]*Ibidem*.
[43]Aquinas, *Summa Theologiae*, I, 7, 2 corp.; I, 14, 1 corp; I, II, 2, 6.

True Infinity, he tells us, in relating itself to itself (position) excludes *otherness* as not identical to it. But this is the production of the *One* and the *Many*. Thus the *One* and the *Many* are based upon the *true infinity*, and are what they are by a relation of negation to it. But this fact sets up a contradiction which must be overcome in a higher principle of unity. And this higher principle reconciling the one and the many and true infinity is that of *Repulsion* and *Attraction*.[44] In this way, Hegel explains, the physical phenomenon of attraction and repulsion are reducible to relation. Atom attracts atom because of the negativity of the *One* and the *Many* with respect to the true infinity, and this is overcome by *Attraction* and *Repulsion* in a higher unity.

And so, in general, the category of Quality is throughout a relational construction. Position, negation and reconciliation, applied at the start to bare being, constitute it. And so by knowing them one can completely understand this category.

3. In the Category of Quantity

The category of Quantity is the negation of that of Quality. Thus negation constitutes it and makes it posterior to Quality. And so again it contains within itself the same constitutive relations.

Hegel tells us that Quantity is subsumed and resolved being-for-self (aufgehobene Fürsichseyn). In so far as it is this, it posits itself as identical to itself (the movement of *position*), and by this position it establishes *pure quantity*. But in so far as it contains the movements of Attraction and Repulsion (which are in it because it is a reconciliation of Quality) it gives rise to the distinction of Continuous and Discrete Quantity.[45] For continuity and discretion in quantity are the negative of pure quantity in itself.

Thus in this case again the category is structured by the application of position and negation, and reaches its term in a higher reconciliating principle, in this case that of Quantitative Ratio.

Yet it is clear that this latter is itself only a relative term and as such points beyond itself to another. This further term Hegel calls that of *Measure*.

[44]*Logik*, I, Cl. 4, p. 200 ff.
[45]*Ibidem*, p. 239.

4. In the Category of Measure

Hegel finds the need for this new term in the conflict resulting within the preceding category. This is a conflict of Quality and Quantity which, although they are separately structured by the same relations, are not united into one while by any proper relation of reconciliation. Their relation is negation. And thus they must be subsumed into a higher principle of unity. Hegel holds that this is done in the category of Measure.[46] By this latter he understands something which is quantitative and qualitative at once but without the limitations of either separate category. And since it unites Determined Being and Quantity, he calls it "specific quantity", i.e. qualified quantity—a quantity which is not *any* quantity nor one simply opposed to quality by negation, but one which is bound to Determined Being.[47]

The relations which structure this category are the same as those we have already seen. For Quantified Being, under the unifying principle of *Ratio*, posits itself as in itself and thus constitutes itself as "specific quantity". It then exteriorizes itself through negation (the external relation to the real principle of measure). And finally it comes to rest in itself through subsumption into a higher principle of unity which Hegel considers to be that of Essence.[48] Thus this category too is relational and terminates in Essence as its point of reconciliation.

5. In the Category of Essence

We shall deal but briefly with the structure of the category of Essence since this has already been fairly thoroughly investigated in the discussion of the category of Relation.

Concerning it Hegel shows that its relational structure is triadic. For it first posits itself in identity, then exteriorizes itself through negation (by which exteriorization Appearance arises), and finally subsumes itself into itself in the higher unit of Actuality.[49]

The first movement of this triad is particularly interesting since Hegel introduces into it the fundamental submovements of the of the essential and the nonessential, mere appearance and reflection—those

---

[46] *Ibidem*, p. 405 ff.
[47] *Ibidem*, p. 417.
[48] *Ibidem*, p. 476 ff.
[49] *Ibidem*, p. 662.

already referred to by Stace as themselves being relations.⁵⁰ This passes into a second movement—that of the Reflective Determinations —with the submovements of "identity", "diversity" and "contradiction", which are clearly distinguished and related to "position", "negation" and "reconciliation".⁵¹ The use of the word "identity" to describe this particular "position" is arbitrary on the part of Hegel. For identity exists long before Essence in the structure of his system. Identity of Essence with itself is only one particular form of this general relation.⁵²

Beyond this second movement of the triad there is a third and reconciling term. This Hegel calls Ground (Grund).⁵³ And it is here that he places the familiar categories of Form and Matter, Form and Content, Form and Essence. In doing this he identifies Ground in the scholastic sense of *ratio cognoscendi* with Ground in the scholastic sense of *ratio essendi*. This is the higher principle which gives rise to the category of Appearance by the same relational structure of position, negation and reconciliation. And through Appearance it then gives rise to the category of Relation.

From what we have now seen it is clear that this category is not the only domain of relation but one of many, and, at that, not the most fundamental one. The most fundamental comes before it and causes it. And besides this there are other domains too. They are found everywhere in the structure of reality and of thought between the two poles of the Absolute and bare Being. For Hegel, the philosophical reflection upon Being is simply the bringing to consciousness of these domains and the understanding of reality and thought through them.

B. The Division of Relation in the Broader Sense

1. The Division in Itself

The analysis which we have now completed reveals that there are a number of distinct relations in the Hegelian hierachy of Being. There is "position" which is the fundamental identity of the related thing to

⁵⁰Stace, *The Philosophy of Hegel*, p. 203.
⁵¹*Logik* I, Gl. 4, p. 535 ff.
⁵²Stace, *The Philosophy of Hegel*, p. 203.
⁵³*Logik*, I, Gl. 4, p. 551 ff.
⁵⁴Aquinas, *Summa Theologiae*, I, 13, 4 corp.; I, 58, 4, ad 2; I, 108, 1 corp.

itself. There is "negation" which is a relationship of opposition to "position".[55] There is "reconciliation" which is a unifying relation having as its lower term the opposition of negation and position, and as its upper one, the unity by which its supports them.[56]

Again, there is "quantitiative relation" or Ratio, and Essential Relation which is the structuring principle of Appearance. Finally there is Absolute Relation which constitutes Substance and Accident, Cause and Effect, and Mutual Interaction.[57]

These different relations have one common *ratio* which Hegel is accustomed to call "Beziehung". They are all "Beziehungen" and their differences are differences of the latter.

This being so their fundamental division separates them into those which are functional in the structuring of all reality and thought, and those which are restricted to particular areas only. The relations which function throughout the entire structure of reality are those of "position", "negation" and "reconciliation". Those which are restricted to particular areas only are the Quantitative Relation, the Essential Relation, and the Absolute Relation". These latter are caused by the former. Quantitative Relation, Essential Relation, and Absolute Relation are simply particular "reconciliations".

A property distinguishing the fundamental relations from these caused ones is their lack of "sides" (Seiten). The distinctions of the less fundamental relations which have sides are the following:

1. Quantitative Relation—has sides which are not independent totalities
2. Essential Relation—has sides which are independent totalities
3. Absolute Relation—has sides which fuse into one another in the unity of a higher reconciliation

2. A Scholastic Interpretation of the Division
a. Of the Relations of Position and Negation

From the scholastic point of view, "position" and "negation" are *relations of reason*, that is to say, ones which are found in things in so far as they are known by human reason. They are not real, that is to say they are not relations found in things independently of reason

---
[55]*Logik* II, Gl. 5, p. 341.
[56]*Logik* I, Gl. 4, pp. 125, 128, 130, 131.
[57]*Ibidem*, p. 696 ff.

although they may have a root in reality causing the mind to take them. "Position" and "negation" pertain formally not to things in themselves but to things as judged by reason.[58]

Discoursing about them Hegel argues that they are identical since they involve the total reference of their terms one to the other. In other words he tells us that since "position" is all that it is by opposition to "negation", it is therefore identical with the latter. This a scholastic could not accept as valid for he himself posits relations which are equally total without identifying their terms. This he does, for example in the case of potency and act, or matter and form. He does not argue that since these are "transcendentally" related one to the other they are identical in their reality.[59]

b. Of the Relation of Reconciliation

The smiliarity of this relation to one which is essential in the doctrine of participation is so close and the texts in which Hegel gives his doctrinal sources for it are so clear that it is quite easy for a scholastic to decide that they are in fact the same. "Reconciliation" seems clearly the same relation as that of the *per se* to the *per participationem*. The Thomist would not however admit this makes the *per se* and the *per participationem* ontologically *identical*. Thus, in theorizing on the ontological structure of created things, he would admit a real distinction of essence and existence in them. From this he would conclude that they are totally relational to each other and, as such, intrinsically opposed—that essence is relationally *opposed* to existence and is therefore that which *is not* of itself existent. This makes it a sort of "negation" of existence. But it does not therefore identify the two. Existence, for the Thomist, is likewise relative to created essence and thus is not sufficient to itself. For this reason both it and essence postulate a third relation to an extrinsic principle whereby they are united. And this third relation is, in the last analysis, one which terminates in pure subsistent Act. It is the "reconciliation" of Hegel but it is not identical to the essence or existence which it unites.

Thus, to paraphrase Hegel, essence contains a negativity (the exclusion of existence) and, in this sense, a contradiction. The contra-

---

[58] Aquinas, *Summa Theologiae*, I, 85, 5, ad 3.
[59] *Ibidem*, I, 3, 8 corp.

diction is "lifted" in the reilation of the compound of essence and existence to *subsistent act*. This paraphrase is, of course, purely formal.[60]

In the traditional picture, then, three relations somewhat similar to those of Hegel are found to be necessary to explain the objects of experience. But they are not of such a nature as to identify the created essence with its First Cause as an identical immanent principle.[61]

c. Of Quantitative Relation

Quantitative Relation, for the scholastic, is "predicamental", that is to say one whose total being consists in its *adesse*. As such it is an "accident" added over and above substantial being with quantity for its foundation. Thus for the scholastic it would more naturally fall into the category of Appearance in the relation of Inner and Outer or into the category of Actuality in the relation of Substance and Accident. Hegel, however, since he reduces ontological relations to rational ones, identifies it with the "quantity" which is found in conception and judgement and therefore places it after predication (Quality).[62]

d. Of Essential Relation

The interpretation of this category from a scholastic point of view is not easy. It is ambiguous under its form of Whole and Part. As such it can be either "predicamental" if it is an accidental whole or "transcendental," if it is "per se". In either case, of course, it is real.

The interpretation of the other two essential relations, on the other hand, is easy. Clearly they are both "transcendental". Force and its Manifestation, Inner and Outer are the relations of the "parts" of a substance to that substance itself, and this is "transcendental."

e. Of Absolute Relation

Absolute relation is likewise ambiguous. Its first movement, that of Substantiality, is clearly "transcendental". But its second and

---

[60]The relations are *formally* the same but their order and explanation are totally different.
[61]Aquinas, *Summa Theologiae*, I, 8, 1.
[62]*Logik* I, Gl. 4, p. 222 ff. J. Maréchal, in *Le Point de Départ de la Métaphysique*, 5 vols. 1923-1926, supports the thesis that individualization or quantification of the concept is by an extrinsic relation and that the failure to realize this is at the source of many modern errors in epistemology. Hegel's quantity is clearly intrinsic rather than extrinsic.

third movements are "predicamental". And all three involve real relations, not rational ones, although Hegel reduces them to the latter as to their ultimate root since he asserts that they arise through "position", "negation" and "reconciliation."

4. Summary

The considerations of this chapter make it clear then that Hegel's doctrine of relation extends far beyond his so-called category of Relation. In fact it encompasses the entire structure of being and thought. And in this broad range Essential Relation is relatively insignificant. "Position", "negation" and "reconciliation" are fundamental. For this reason, we must now take a closer look at these structural principles of the Hegelian system.

CHAPTER IV

THE FUNDAMENTAL RELATIONS

The study of Hegel's text in the preceding chapter makes it inductively certain that the basic relations for him are those of *position*, *negation* and *reconciliation*. These are the ones which he always uses to structure thought or being.

Thus he applies them to being at the beginning of the *Logic* and asserts that they are the only ones which he can use:

> It is therefore not permissible to employ other determined mediations (bestimmte Vermittelungen) here and to conceive of Being and Nothing in any sort of relation (Verhältniss),—this transition (Uebergehen) is not yet a relation (Verhältniss). It is therefore unacceptable (unstatthaft) to say: Nothing is the ground of Being; or Being is the ground of Nothing;—Nothing is the cause of Being and so forth . . . The kind of relation (Beziehung) cannot be further determined without at the same time determining further the related sides (Seiten). The interconnection of ground (Grund) and consequence (Folge) and so forth no longer has mere Being and Nothing for its sides, which it binds together, but explicitly (ausdrücklich) Being which is ground . . .[1]

The generality of this conclusion permits us to include within it the further qualification that it is not permissible to conceive of Being and Nothing as *whole* and *part*, as *force* and *manifestation*, as *inner* and *outer*. The Essential Relationship, of which these are movements, does not apply to Being so immediately.

Hegel asserts that in order for the relation of Ground and Consequence to be applied to Being, it must first itself be explicitly structured as Ground (Grund).[2] This occurs only in the category of Essence. And therefore until the structure of that category is first posited, the relation of Ground and Consequence cannot be applied.

[1] *Logik* I, Gl. 4, pp. 115, 116.
[2] *Ibidem.*

The text cited is interesting also for its interplay of the two words "Verhältniss" and "Beziehung". "Verhältniss" is reserved for the realm of Essence. "Beziehung" is applied to the sphere of Being. This is consistent with Hegel's dictum in the *Encyclopedia of the Philosophical Sciences*:

> In the sphere of Essence (Wesen) relativity (Relativität) is the dominant determination (die herrschende Bestimmung). In the sphere of Being (Seyns), Identity is the immediate reference (Beziehung) to itself, and the Negative, the pure Otherness (Anderseyn).[3]

The relations of *position, negation* and *reconciliation* are therefore the most fundamental ones because they apply to the initial structure of reality.[4] But they also apply to its entire structure whereas "Verhältniss" applies only to restricted categories of it. The text cited gives the reason why this is so.[5] It is because "Verhältniss" as opposed to simple "Beziehung" supposes a further modification and determination of its terms, i.e. supposes a structured Being and not Being or Nothing purely and simply.[6]

The application of these fundamental relations to every level of Being can be documented without any difficulty in Hegel's works. It is, in fact, the whole point of his system. Every level of Being is simply an "overcoming" of conflicts on a lower level, that is to say it is the assumption of lower oppositions into unity. And the point of the Hegelian speculations is to determine exactly what it is that is to be *overcome*, and what it is that achieves this. It is the determination of these that serves to define any particular level of Being for him.

For this reason it is necessary in any attempt to understand his thought that one first determine how he conceives of *"position"*, *"negation"* and *"reconciliation."*

A. How Hegel Conceives of Position

In an early text, Hegel defines the *positive* in this way:

> The positive is by nature (der Natur nach) prior to the negative; or, Aristotle puts it: the social group is prior by nature to the individual.[7]

---

[3] *Encyclopädie*, Gl. 6, p. 69.
[4] *Ibidem.*
[5] *Ibidem.*
[6] *Ibidem.*
[7] *Wissenschaftliche Behandlungsarten des Naturrechts*, Gl. 1, pp. 510, 511.

This, he explains, is because the individual, cut off from the group, is not independent and self sufficient. By nature he is a potential part of it and thus a possibility of its universal spirit (allgemeinen Geistes).[8] When he is actually a part of it, then it is *in* him. But as a pure possibility for this, he is then *not* spirit. And thus in him the positive is prior to the negative by nature.[9]

Nevertheless it is not independent of the latter. For, as Hegel tells us in the *Phenomenology of Mind*

> The positive *is* only in so far as it is by reference to the negative (nur als Beziehung auf ein Negatives) or the positive is *in itself* the distinction (der Unterschied) of itself, just as the negative is (wie eben so das Negative).[10]

This is an extremely important formula since Hegel draws fundamental principles from it. It asserts that the positive has existence or entity or meaning only through relation to the negative. From this it concludes that relation to the negative essentially constitutes the posiive, that is to say that its essence is "to be relative to the negative." But this signifies that the positive *has* the negative *within* its essence, or in Hegel's words that it "has its distinction from the negative within it." Therefore, Hegel concludes, it and the negative are the same. This is basic to all of his dialectical constructions.

We have already seen how he attempts to establish this principle in the beginning of the *Logic*.[11] There he argues to it from the lack of differentiation in pure Being which makes it Nothing and thus makes the positive and the negative the same. In the present text he argues to the same conclusion from the relational structure of position and negation in themselves, asserting that since they are all that they are is by relation to each other, they are the same. This states, when generalized so that its universal import can be seen, that whatever is all that it is by relation to another term is the same as that term. So formulated it is a principle from which Hegel continually argues as in the present text. Obviously this is a key point to his thought on the nature of relation. Later on we shall offer another reason for his acceptance of it. For the moment let us notice only that he does accept it as fundamental.

[8]*Ibidem*, p. 511.
[9]*Ibidem*.
[10]*Phänomenologie des Geistes*, Gl. 2, p.
[11]*Logik* I, Gl. 4, p. 88 ff.

Again he tells us that

> This likeness with itself reflected into itself, which contains in itself the relation (Beziehung) to dissimilarity (auf die Ungleichheit) is the positive.[12]

Thus he holds that the positive is a likeness to itself, i.e. a relation in which it is both beginning and term—a relation of identity or similarity. It is also *reflected* into itself. This statement may seem strange if we do not take into account the function of identity with respect to the relation of similarity. Identity is that in which similarity subsists. And thus both position and negation, in so far as they are identities, contain similarity and therefore reflect into themselves.

Hegel's thought on this point seems superficially similar to that of St. Thomas.

> But the composition of the intellect is a sign of identity (signum identitatis) in those things which are composed. Our intellect does not compose by saying "man is whiteness"; but rather by saying that "man is white" or that he is a "thing having whiteness": for "man" and 'thing having whiteness" are identical in reality . . . And therefore our intellect composes according to the *ratio* of identity . . .[13]

The judgement, according to this text, is an identification involving no distinction in reality for the things identified.[14] It begins in real unity; passes into conceptual diversity;; and finally ends in mental composition.[15] This structure is not however for St. Thomas the ontological structure of the reality. Nevertheless what he says of its logical relations helps to clarify Hegel's notion that "position" and "negation" are *reflected* into themselves. This means no more than that they are rooted in identity. And since affirmation is also dissimilar to negation it must be similar to itself. Thus it must be a likeness to itself reflected into itself.[16]

For this reason, then, "position" and "negation" are independent sides of an opposition(selbstständige gewordenen Seiten des Gegensatzes).[17] But this must not be understood to mean that they have the

---

[12]*Logik*, I, Gl. 4, p. 526.
[13]Aquinas, *Summa Theologiae*, I, 85, 5 and 3; I, 13, 12 corp.
[14]*Ibidem*.
[15]*Ibidem*.
[16]*Logik*, I, Gl. 4, p. 526.
[17]*Ibidem*, p. 526.

sort of independence which is found in Essential Relation. True, this latter is like position and the negation in that it too involves reflection into self through reflection into its opposite.[18] But its sides are *totalities*.[19] The sides of the opposition between positive and negative, on the contrary, are *partialities* having no more unity than that of their negative oneness.[20] They are bound by a relation so simple that its meager terminal entity suffices for them and, thus, for all being.

In the *Philosophy of Religion* Hegel gives some interesting insights into the nature of the positive. He tells us that it is in itself lacking in rationality.[21] What is positive by nature (seiner Natur nach positiv) is irrational (Vernunftlose).[22] For this reason religion appears at first to be irrational since it is first *positive*. But it cannot long remain such since it would then be a mere thing of representation (Vorstellung) or recollection (Gedächtnisses).[23] This cannot be because the positive is by essence *to the negative* and therefore must develop into the latter.

The assertion of the "irrationality" of the positive cannot be complete without the additional assertion of the relation of *reconciliation*. Since this latter has the same relation to things it reconciles as that which the *Nous* has to intelligible things in Neo-platonic doctrine, that which, among the latter, is furthest removed from it has the least intelligibilty. *Position*, in the Hegelian scheme, is this. And thus it is the "least intelligible" or the "least similar" to Nous and, in this sense, the irrational. For the same reason it is also "arbitrary" and "contingent", whereas the concept (reconciling it with negation) is "truly free".[24]

Such, in general, is Hegel's doctrine on the *positive*. It is prior by nature to the *negative* but, nevertheless, essentially correlative to the latter. It is "reflected into itself" since it is a movement within identity. Therefore it is a likeness to itself which is reflected into itself. These relations define it.

---

[18]*Ibidem*, p. 640.
[19]*Ibidem*.
[20]*Ibidem*.
[21]*Philosophie der Religion*, Gl. 16, p. 200.
[22]*Ibidem*.
[23]*Ibidem*.
[24]*Ibidem*.

B. How Hegel Conceives of Negation

The correlative of the positive and therefore that which is in good part explained by the latter, is the negative. Hegel has a vast doctrine on this movement of thought. It will suffice for our purposes to deal here with only a small part of this.

Negation, he tells us, is quality associated with a denial (mit einer Verneinung behaftet). Thus it is to be understood as Bradley understands it, that is to say, as a relation associated intimately with a qualification.[25] As such it clearly is in the category of Quality. For it is the cause of Nothing and of Determined Being.[26] And these are, for Hegel, the heart of Quality.

Moreover, it is distinguished into a first and a second manifestation. The first we have already seen. The second is that of the "negation of a negation" (Negation der Negation).[27] It is *absolute negativity* relative to which the first is only *partial*. Moreover, it is to the first as the concrete to the abstract.[28]

In its first manifestation negation may be taken as a simple determination (einfache Bestimmung) but, in its truth (ihrer Wahrheit nach), it is a relation (eine Beziehung). For it *is negative* but *of the positive* and therefore includes the latter.[29] In this argument we meet again Hegel's principle: if a thing is all that it is by relation to another, it is identical with that other and therefore includes the latter in its being. On the basis of this principle Hegel concludes that the first negative is identical with the positive.[30] For this reason he characterizes it in much the same way as he does the positive in the *Phenomenology of Mind,* asserting that just as the positive *is* only through relation to the negative and therefore contains its distinction from the negative within itself, so also is this true of the negative.[31] Therefore this latter is a dissimilarity (Ungleichheit) containing within itself a relation (Beziehung) to its own non being (Nichtseyn), which relation is that of similarity (Gleichheit) found in and constitutive of the positive.[32]

[25] *Logik* I, Cl. 4, p. 125.
[26] *Ibidem.*
[27] *Logik* I, Cl. 4, p. 130.
[28] *Ibidem.*
[29] *Logik* II, Cl. 5, p. 341.
[30] *Logik* I, Cl. 4, p. 541.
[31] *Phänomenologie des Geistes,* Cl. 2, p. 124.
[32] *Logik* I, Cl. 4, p. 526.

The purely positive, he then concludes, is irrational, and the purely negative, empty. So he tells us in the *Aesthetics*:

> For the merely negative (das nur Negative) is in general in itself flat and stale (matt und platt) and therefore either leaves us empty (leer) or repulses us (stösst uns zurück) . . .[33]

This statement, although somewhat poetical in expression, has general metaphysical import. Hegel concludes from it that the devil is an aesthetically useless figure (eine schlechte aesthetisch unbrauchbare Figur).

In the *History of Philosophy*, applying the same idea, he tells us that the moment of negativity is immanent in the philosophy of Heraclitus which therefore deals with the concept of the entirety of Philosophy.[34] It is clear from this remark that he considers the structuring function of negation to be so fundamental that without it philosophy is a barren positivism lacking reason.[35]

For him, therefore, negation may be taken as a simple determination or limitation, but more properly (i.e. in its *truth*) it should be taken as a relation since it is essentially *of* the positive. Because of this, too, it is a relation of dissimilarity since it is opposed to the positive, which is a relation of similarity to itself. The negative thus contains within itself a reference to its own non being.

This is Bradley's conviction, too, when he asserts:

> And the main point here is this, that all negation is relative. Negation, whatever else it is, is repulsion not absolute but from a subject formed by distinction within reality.[36]

Thus it is not pure and absolute opposition for him but, rather, opposition to a definite term—the "subject formed by distinction within reality" i.e. formed by the introduction of the relations of identity and diversity into the undifferentiated content of the beginning of all thought.[37] And because he holds it to be this, he then concludes that it is not "a mere refusal to entertain the unmeaning but rather a determined denial of the unintelligible."[38]

---

[33] *Aesthetik* I, Gl. 12, p. 301.
[34] *Geschichte der Philosophie* I, Gl. 17, p. 351.
[35] *Ibidem*.
[36] Bradley, *Essays on Truth and Reality*, p. 40.
[37] *Ibidem*.
[38] *Ibidem*.

Bosanquet further advances these considerations by asserting that they do not imply the psychological precedence of a positive judgment to every negative one. They mean solely that the relationality, which constitutes the negative judgment, is such as to make the positive prior by nature.[39]

It is helpful in this context to refer again to the Thomistic notion of the judgment. This is a mental composition of different concepts concerning one and the some real thing. Thus it first and fundamentally presupposes the unity of reality. It then supposes diversification of concepts. These it synthesizes by identification, either under the form of affirmation or of negation, the latter being founded always upon the former. In so far as this is the case, the judgment may be regarded as a "reflection into itself". And, for Hegel, it is that sort of reflection into self which rests upon "dissimilarity to the positive".[40]

It is clear that much of this Hegelian doctrine from the purely logical point of view is not new. It is no more than the generally accepted teaching on the relations of position and negation. But where it identifies the one with the other, it is the new and unusual doctrine of *reconciliation*.

C. How Hegel Conceives of Reconciliation

1. The Existence of this Relation

That a "higher form of being" in which position and negation are united into one actually exists, Hegel does not doubt. Indeed, he thinks this an intuition.

> It is so simple an insight (so einfach die Einsicht ist) that the negation of a negation is something positive that proud reason (der stolze Verstand) pays no attention to it although attention should surely be paid to it because of the universality of such determinations. For they have infinite extension (unendliche Ausdehnung) and universal application.[41]

2. The Nature of This Relation

In the text cited Hegel does not reveal his entire hand but simply calls the attention of the reader to the necessity of considering the significance of the *negation of negation*. The average reader responds

---
[39] *Logik* I, Cl. 4, p. 276 ff.
[40] *Logic* I, Cl. 4, p. 526.
[41] *Logik* I, Cl. 4, p. 115.

to this just about as Hegel anticipates and assumes that it is a return to an original positive statement. But this is not its meaning for Hegel. He has a totally different insight into it.

How different this insight is he clearly shows in a striking passage from his *Philosophy of Religion*. In treating of the religion of enigma (des Räthsels) he asserts that an essential element of this is the movement whereby God resurrects Himself (sich wiederherstellt, aufersteht).[42] This is an action of Spirit (Geist) which is free and therefore necessarily contains the movement of negation (enthält das Moment der Negation).[43] But, the crucial statement posits, the *negation of negation* is the return into self (das Zurückkehren in sich) and the Spirit is the eternal return into self (das ewige Zurückgehen in sich).[44] This is to understand the *negation of negation* not as a simple return to an original positive affirmation but as an evolution into the higher intellectual knowledge of the Platonic and Aristotelian *Nous*. It is the exercizing of the proper activity of this *Nous*. And since the latter knows by turning into itself, so the *negation of a negation* is the return (Zurückgehen) into self.

There can be no doubt that this is Hegel's interpretation of it. The text cited is perfectly clear, and there are indefinitely many others besides. But perhaps the most striking corroboration is given by Hegel's citation at the end of the *Encyclopedia* of the Aristotelian passage on the life of the Nous which is the First Cause. It is quoted as a summation of the treatise (at the very end) and without commentary (that is to say, without qualification):

> Now thinking in itself is concerned with that which is in the highest sense best. And thought thinks itself through participation in the object of thought . . . . so that thought and the object of thought are the same.[45]

From the position which he thus gives this famous passage in the *Encyclopedia*, it is clear that Hegel intends not only to make its thought his own but to present it as a resumé. There can be no question, then, but that the Aristotelian and Platonic *Nous* is the same as the Hegelian *negation of negation*. This is not to assert that the two are identical in every way. Grégoire points to at least one

[42] *Philosophie der Religion*, Gl. 15, p. 451.
[43] *Ibidem*.
[44] *Ibidem*.
[45] Aristotle, *Metaphysics* XII, 7, 1072 b 18 ff.

significant difference between them: Aristotle thinks that he sees the activity of the Supreme Spirit only "as in a mirror darkly"; Hegel, on the other hand, thinks that he sees it "face to face."[46]

3. The Importance of This Relation

The importance of reconciliation in Hegel's mind is clearly stated in an illuminating "Anmerkung" in the *Logic*.

> *Reconciliation* (Aufheben) and the *reconciled* (das Aufgehobene) ... is one of the most important concepts of philosophy, a fundamental determination (eine Grundbestimmung) which is met everywhere, and whose meaning must be definitely grasped and particularly distinguished from that of Nothing.[47]

That which is "reconciled", the text states, is not thereby rendered nothing. This is an insight of universal application.

Its doctrinal content is evident. "Reconciliation" is one of the most important concepts in philosophy. For this reason it must be clearly grasped and sharply distinguished from the concept of "nothing". That which it "reconciles" it does not destroy Hegel adds to this that the "reconciled" is, in the full sense, the "ideal". He thus intimately associates "reconciliation" with *Nous* and its object. "Reconciliation" is the proper activity of *Nous* and the "reconciled" is its proper object.

4. A Scholastic Interpretation of This Relation

Hegel's exhortation that we attempt "definitely to grasp" this relation is sufficient justification for introducing at this point some further considerations from traditional thought. According to this doctrine, Hegel's theory takes relations of reason, i.e ones which exist formally in thought and not in things in themselves, and attempts to combine them with real relations. For it attempts to unite the rational structure of "affirmation" and "negation" with the real structure of the *participating* and the *per se*. This is his dialectic. He clearly shows this in his conception of the relation of the Nous (Eternal Spirit) to "reconciled" things as a "negation of a negation"

---

[46] Grégoire, *Etudes Hegeliennes*, p. 46, footnote.
[47] *Logik* I, Gl. 4, p. 120.

which is, at the same time, a "Zurückgehen" or Reflection (the "omnis sciens qui scit essentiam suam est rediens ad essentiam reditione completa" of the tradition as expressed in the commentary of St. Thomas on the *Liber De Causis*[48]), as in the text already cited from the *Philosophy of Religion*.[49] But this is to identify the relational structure proper to things as they are thought by reason with that which is found in them in so far as they are ontologically dependent upon *Nous*.

This being so, it is crucial to the understanding of Hegel's thought that we understand what is meant by "participation."[50] Put in the simplest terms, it means that there are two levels of being, one which is *per se*, or of itself, and without dependence upon another (though this may be understood as in a *particular* order of being only); and one which is *by participation*, that is to say, which possesses a property or a quality by sharing it from the former.

That this latter is essentially *dependent* can be established in many ways. St. Thomas argues to it from the fact that "having by participation" supposes a composition in the participating thing of that which *receives* a participated form, and the *form* itself. But, if this is so, then such a thing is an intrinsic *diversity* out of which, as such, unity cannot come.[51] Therefore it must find its unity not from itself but from something else outside. And this external cause must be ultimately *one* and *simple*. This is the *per se* which does not *have form* or *act* but *is* it.[52]

In the last analysis, then, a *participating thing* supposes a *per se* which causes it. If we should cut it off from the latter, we would bring about its destruction. For it could not then maintain itself. In order to be it must maintain its relation to the *per se*.[53]

One can clearly see in this reasoning a ground for Hegel's assertion that the "reconciling" principle "supports" the inner contradictions of the "reconciled" things. For *participating things* are unable to support themselves solely by their mutual interior relations.

---

[48]Aquinas, *In Librum De Causis Expositio*, Prop. XV, no. 301 ff. (ed. Pera, p. 88 ff.).
[49]*Philosophie der Religion*, Gl. 15, p. 451.
[50]Aquinas, *op. cit.* Prooemium (ed. Pera, p. 4 ff.) and passim.
[51]Aquinas, *Summa Theologiae*, I, 65, 1, corp.; I, 11, 3, corp.
[52]*Ibidem*.
[53]*Ibidem*.

The *per se* moreover, is simple, but the *participating things* are *composed* and *many*. As many, they mutually limit one another so that they differ in perfection.[54] And thus they have a perfection which is increased only through their multiplication (Hegel's "false infinity"). But the *per se* contains all of its perfection without any limitation (Hegel's "true infinity") or contradiction. It is a sort of harmony, as the soul was conceived to be by the early Greek philosophers.[55] For it harmonizes in itself the movements and qualities of body without their limitations.[56]

The number of things, which depend upon this *per se*, is infinite. This infinity seems to the yet uncritical mind to be the embodiment of the notion. Actually it is only an imperfect form. The perfect form is found in the *per se*. The simple richness of this cause exceeds by far the indefinite quantitative richness of participating things and contains the latter without loss of simplicity.[57] The relation between this doctrine and that of "false" and "true infinity" is again too close to be purely coincidental. "True infinity" (or the "concrete universal") is quite obviously the *"per se"* of the tradition.[58] This is the obvious sense of Hegel's citation of Aristotle.[59]

It is clearly justifiable then, to understand the Hegelian dialectic as a mixture of the doctrine of the *Nous* (the *per se—per participationem*) and the Logic of rational relations involved in affirmation and negation. Hegel, in this interpretation, makes his dialectical triad from *Nous* as one extreme of reality, and *bare being* as the other. He then endeavors to connect the two through the relational structures which each separately has. This is the root of his difficult notion of *reconciliation* (Aufgehobenheit). His procedure in forming it is quite intelligible. He must show that the relations of *participation* are those of *affirmation* and *negation*. He does this by observing that the finiteness of *participating things* is a negation, and that the *per se* stands above this as negating or excluding its limitation. It is a *negation of negation*. Negation and original affirmation thus become the structure of participation and of the dialectic. And since the *Nous* lives

---

[54] Aquinas, Summa Theologiae, I, 2, 3 corp.
[55] Aristotle, *On the Soul*, 1, 4, 407 b 26 ff.
[56] *Ibidem*.
[57] Aquinas, Summa Theologiae, I, 7, 1 ff.
[58] Encyclopädie II, Gl. 9, p. 46; Aquinas, *In Librum De Causis Expositio*, Prop. II ff. (ed. Pera, p. 14 ff.).
[59] *Encyclopädie* III, Gl. 10, pp. 475, 476.

by reflection into itself, the *negation of negation* becomes "reflection into self". And the self-consciousness of Spirit becomes the upper term of the dialectic which the lower positive term attempts to reach by evolution.

This, of course, reverses the traditional order between the *per se* and the *per participationem*. The *per se*, in traditional thought, comes first and the *per participationem* follows on it. Hegel inverts this order since he takes the abstract ratio of being as first, and then develops the relations upward from it. This seems to him to conform to experience, as he theorizes in the *Phenomenology of Mind*. Consciousness, as a human experience, seems to develop upwards from abstract being rather than downwards from pure self consciousness. This is why he conceives of it as a passage from a lower to a higher, and as a "lifting" or "resolution" or "reconciliation". From the formal point of view, it is simply a relation. From the dynamic point of view, it is the coming into being of that which does not previously exist, that is to say, of the "*per se*", and since this does not contain the limitations (and therefore negations and contradictions) of the participating things, it is a "harmony" and a "resolution" and a "lifting" of negation.

It is clear why Hegel asserts that this "reconciliation" does not destroy contradiction. For just as the *per se* supports the *per participationem* without destroying the relative opposition of its parts, so "reconciliation" supports contradiction.[60]

The term "lifting" seems to suggest that this is not the case. It seems to signify a *removal* or *elimination*. Hegel feels that this is not the case. The word does not really mean this even in common usage.

> "Overcoming (Aufheben) has a two-fold meaning in common speech: that of preservation (erhalten) and that of cessation (aufhören)."[61]

This causes him to feel a certain satisfaction with common German speech which thus manifests not only a practical meaning but also a speculative one. With understandable German pride, he points this out as a sign of superiority to Latin. Latin expresses the same concepts by the word "tollere" which has a double meaning, as is indicated in Cicero's pun "tollendum esse Octavium", but which does not go so far as to mean preservation (Erhalten), stopping short with the lesser

[60]*Logik* I, Gl. 4, p. 120.
[61]*Ibidem.*

meaning of "lifting" (Emporheben).[62] If it went further, then it would signify, as does the German word, that the "negation" is not dissolution but preservation.[63]

For this reason, he concludes, the *negation of negation* is not a mere return to an original affirmation. It is, rather, a movement to a higher principle of unity.[64] And, as such, it is one of the fundamental insights of philosophy.[65] He quotes with pleasure Aristotle's judgement of Anaxagoras who, first among the Greeks, discovered it in this. Anaxagoras was like a sober man among drunks.[66] The insight is deplorably missing in Spinoza.[67] Spinoza knows the primary negative, since he holds that everything which is not God is His negation.[68] But when he says "omnis determinatio est negatio"—he expresses only the primary negation.[69] He fails to express the "negation of negation" which is a higher "position".[70] This failure is his chief defect (Mangel).[71] It is the chief defect of the Eleatic notion of "being" too—an oriental intuition (morgenländische Anschauung) which found its first utterance in occidental thought through Spinoza.[72]

There is a text in the *Encyclopedia* where Hegel gives the same etymology of "aufheben" but draws a different conclusion from it. Common language, he asserts, contains two meanings, the one speculative and the other practical. This should not surprise us since speech manifests not only practical but also speculative Spirit, which stands above mere understanding. And thus, where mere understanding presents us with an either/or (Entweder/Oder) situation, speculative Spirit reconciles these opposites in a higher unity.[73]

5. Confirmation of This Interpretation by Criticism

The validity of this interpretation of "reconciliation" can be confirmed by criticizing the arguments which Hegel gives to prove that

[62] *Ibidem.*
[63] *Ibidem.*
[64] *Philosophie der Religion,* Gl. 15, p. 451.
[65] *Log k* I, Gl. 4, p. 120.
[66] *Geschichte der Philosophie* I, Gl. 17, p. 397. "Anaxagoras ist wie ein Nüchterner unter Trunkenen erschienen."
[67] *Geschichte der Philosophie,* Gl. 19, p. 374 ff.
[68] *Ibidem,* p. 375.
[69] *Ibidem.*
[70] *Ibidem.*
[71] *Ibidem.*
[72] *Ibidem,* p. 376.
[73] *Encyclopädie* I, Gl. 8, p. 229.

position is *negation*. These are theoretically weak and cannot therefore be supposed to be the prime cause of his conviction.

The arguments are two:
- a. That abstract being is so totally lacking in all determination as to be identical with absolute nothing (thus "position" and "negation" are the same);
- b. That the positive and the negative, since they are all that they are by relation one to the other, are therefore identical.

Neither the one nor the other is truly conclusive. It is improbable, then, that they were the root motive for Hegel's doctrine.

The first argument is given in the *Logic*. Hegel, wishing to show that Being and Nothing are identified in Becoming, argues that pure being is absolutely indetermined and, therefore, a vacuity in which nothing can be seen. But this means that it is identical with Nothing. Therefore, Being and Nothing are the same.

The weakness of this argument is patent and Hegelian commentators, while they recognize that it suggests some sort of similarity between the vacuity of Being and that of Nothing, do not unanimously admit that it proves identification. Sartre holds that it does not noting that the vacuity is not the same. The emptiness of *bare being* is an absence of all determinations but the emptiness of *nothing* is an *absence of being*.[74] Grégoire tries to answer this by distinguishing kinds of *being* and of *nothing*, holding then that Hegel identifies not *being* and *nothing* as such, but *indetermined* being and *indetermined* nothing.[75] Whatever may be the validity of this defense it shows, at the very least, that the argument of Hegel is not clear and convincing. This bolsters the rejection of it as the point of departure for Hegel's thought. This was, in part, a reinterpretation of *negation* in terms of a previous insight into the function of *Nous* and of the *per se*.

The second argument is likewise weak. It reasons that if a thing is all that it is by relation to another, then it is identical with that other. Clearly this is not cogent. Thomists, who deal familiarly with the same sort of situation in transcendental relations, would not identify their terms.[76] They might therefore reasonably conclude that the force of Hegel's conviction does not flow from this argument,

---

[74]Sarte, *L'être et le néant*, p. 51.
[75]Grégoire, *Études Hégéliennes*, p. 107 footnote.
[76]*Ibidem*; Aquinas, *Summa Theologiae*, I, 65, 1 corp.

but from something else. This latter could only be the doctrine of the *Nous*.

D. Summary

In brief, then, Hegel pictures reality as a structure composed of basic relations and their terms. The relations are three:

1. position;
2. negation;
3. reconciliation.

Their extreme terms are two:

1. Bare Being;
2. Absolute Spirit.

Position and *negation* are *united* in the common root of *identity* (by reason of which they are said to be reflections into themselves), and *separated* by their mutual opposition. But *position is*, in fact, *negation*, and *negation* is *position*. This situation of conflict is supported and sustained by *reconciliation*.

Reconciliation, in Hegel's doctrine, is easily traced to ancient sources. He himself admits as much in numerous passages. It is the activity of *Nous*, of the *per se* supporting the *per participationem*, in Aristotle, Plato and Neo-platonic tradition. It is the Ideal of Pure Reason in Kant and the Ego of Fichte and Schelling.

Hegel attempts to interpret this relation in terms of *negation*, making it a *negation* of *negation*. In doing this he mixes together the real and the rational. This leads him to attribute to "reconciliation" those properties which make it so difficult to understand: that of being a "true infinity" and a "resolution of contradiction without the destruction of the parts involved in the latter" and a "reflection into self." For if "reconciliation" is an activity akin to that of the *Nous*, and if the activity of the latter is one of self-consciousness (therefore of reflection into self), then "reconciliation" must be "reflection into self."

The two poles between which he operates are those of *Bare Being* and *Absolute Spirit*. The former is an absolute point of departure for rational thought. The latter, in the traditional doctrine, is the absolute point of departure for all that is, since the consciousness of self of the Absolute Spirit is the root of the divine creativity.

With these two extremes, then, and the given relations, Hegel is convinced that he has the principles of thought and reality, by which he can reconstruct any content. Nothing can conceal itself from him. All is transparent. This is the conviction which he confided to his students:

> The fast-bound substance of the universe has no power within it capable of withstanding the courage of man's knowledge: it must give way before him, and lay bare before his eyes, and for his enjoyment, its riches and its depths.[77]

The enthusiasm of these words cooled considerably as they were read by subsequent commentators and submitted to closer scrutiny. This we shall see in the next chapter.

---

[77]Baillie, *Phenomenology of Mind*, p. 40.

CHAPTER V

THE TREATMENT OF RELATION BY LATER PHILOSOPHERS

A. Introduction

1. The Importance of the Doctrine for post-Hegelian Commentators

Hegel thought that his doctrine of relation was the key to the structure of reality. By applying it, he would allow nothing in nature or mind to escape his understanding.[1] Its importance was far reaching. No wonder then that post-Hegelian commentators should fasten upon it as fundamental: that Lasson, Schilling-Wollny, Heimann, Dürr, Hyppolite, Coreth, Grégoire and so many others should be of one mind in holding it rather than qualities to be the essential element in the dialectic[2]

It is not surprising either that all should recognize "reconciliation" or "overcoming" as most important, nor that they should find this a strange relation, difficult to understand, and, for some, a sort of *mystical insight*.

Hyppolite feels this way about it. The Hegelian interpretation of infinity in the Jena *Logic* is a mystical image.[4] True, it is bolstered by an unusual and original *conceptual* framework,[5] but this is not its source. Its true source is an ancient mystical current.[6]

For McTaggart, too, this is the case. "Reconciliation is a mystical insight". He is not surprised that it should be since he regards *mysticism* as a powerful influence in all of modern philosophy. This is a

---
[1]Baillie, op. cit., p. 40.
[2]Coreth, *op. cit.*, p. 25.
[3]*Ibidem*.
[4]Jean Hyppolite, *Études sur Marx et Hegel*, p. 14.
[5]*Ibidem*, p. 17.
[6]*Ibidem*.

fact which he thinks not sufficiently understood so that its influence on Hegel has not been seen.[7] By *mysticism* he means an insight "into a greater unity in the universe than that which is recognized in ordinary experience, or in science". It is a conviction that one can come into closer "and more direct relation with what is known than can be done in ordinary discourse".[8] The *greater unity* is had in the resolution of contradiction; the *closer* insight, in the perception of the intrinsic relations which structure reality.

That Hegel is mystical in this sense can hardly be doubted. That he is thus in continuity with an ancient current is probable enough. He himself makes this abundantly clear all throughout his works. We need recall only the passage already quoted from the *Encyclopedia*,[9] which shows at least that he is far from denying his debt to the past— to Aristotle, Plato and Neo-platonism, Spinoza, Boehme and to all who may be said, in the sense of McTaggart, to embody a mystical tradition.

But his conceptualization of this is a peculiar addition, as Hyppolite maintains, and its key element is *relation*.[10] Before Kant, in the period beginning with Descartes, this played a limited role in solving the problem of knowledge.[11] With Kant, it became the key to a "philosophy of law", that is to say to a philosophy of regularized determinations.[12] With Hegel, it became the structuring principle for the entire content of experience both subjectively and objectively.[13] It is not surprising, then, that it should characterize Hegel's doctrine as a "relational structure" (Beziehungsgefüge)[14] and that post-Hegelian commentators should recognize this fact.

2. The Inadequacy of the Treatment of Relation in the Commentators.

It is surprising, though, that in spite of their convictions, the post-Hegelian commentators should treat of relation so inadequately. Coreth points this out, that, despite universal agreement among post-Hegelians that relation is the fundamental doctrine, they have not yet

---
[7] McTaggart, *Philosophical Studies*, pp. 46, 47.
[8] *Ibidem*.
[9] Chapter 4, footnote no. 45.
[10] Jean Hyppolite, *op. cit.*, p. 17.
[11] *Ibidem*.
[12] *Ibidem*.
[13] *Ibidem*, p. 18.
[14] Coreth, *op. cit.*, p. 24.

given it the close attention and the penetrating investigation which it deserves.[15] In fact, they have given it no attention at all save for Bradley, who makes it the point of departure in his speculations.[16]

The reason for this neglect of the problem, according to Coreth, is the fact that the doctrine of relation has scarcely been studied in modern non-scholastic thought.[17] Peirce and many logicians have written on it but no metaphysician has done it justice. Modern thought, as a consequence, offers nothing to compare with the sophisticated scholastic teaching and its distinction betwees rational and real relations, between predicamental and transcendental ones. And even when something of this doctrine has been proposed, it has been a derivation from the scholastic. Husserl's doctrine of "intentionality" is an example of this.[18]

3. The Results of This Inadequacy

Modern commentators, then, confronted with the variety of relations employed by Hegel in the structure of his system, have been at a loss for an adequate interpretation of them. They have tended to reduce them all to one univocal *ratio* and to consider their distinctions unimportant. From this limiting point of departure they have reached contradictory conclusions, not suspecting that the differentiation of the *ratio* of relation would obviate this difficulty. Small wonder, in this situation, that many of them have been driven to attribute Hegel's "reconciliation" to a "mystical insight". They do not want to hold that it is false, but they can find no reasonable explanation for it.

Some, failing in this way to distinguish the generic *ratio* of relation from specific forms, throw up their hands in despair. Nicolai Hartmann finds the diversity and richness of the dialectic (chiefly in "reconciliation"), such that it can have *no* unity. What unity could there be in a relation so radically diverse? Its form is everywhere different. It is a hundreds "dialectics" *not even two* of which can be reduced to the same formal *ratio*. The dialectic, he then concludes, cannot be pre-analyzed nor explained in terms of a unit genus. Any attempt to

---

[15] *Ibidem.*
[16] *Ibidem.*
[17] *Ibidem.*
[18] Maritain, *"Notes sur la connaissance"* Rivista di filosofia neo-scolastica, January 1932, pp. 13-23.

do this reduces it to an a priori and extrinsic formula foreign to that to which it is applied.[19]

This conclusion is one extreme. The opposite would be this, that the Hegelian dialectic is completely and everywhere one. Their deficient doctrine of relation tends to make consistent thinkers embrace either the former position, or the latter. A mediating position, such as the scholastic notion of "proportional unity", which gives sense to both extremes and, at the same time, reconciles them in one mediating principle is inconceivable. Yet only the flexibility of this point of view allows one see to unity and diversity in the Hegelian dialectic.

It has the unity and diversity of *proportional analogy*. Moderns, who reject Hartmann's extreme position, but have no such doctrine at their disposal, are hard put to justify themselves.[20] Somewhat vaguely they point to the similarities in the dialectic and minimize its dissimilarities. Or, when these are too clear to admit of being overlooked, they attribute them to a particular misapplication.[21] This eliminates the problem by suppressing evidence.

In general, such reasoning from a generic and univocal notion of relation leads to vague if not erroneous conclusions. This result, however, is made possible because of the peculiarity of relation that it alone, of all the categories, is of itself neither real nor rational.[22] This means that it may be discussed without an ontological commitment. But such a generic discussion will not give an adequate insight into the specific relations of Hegel's dialectic. This is, for Coreth, the reason which prevents the moderns from understanding the dialectic. A scholastic, unimpeded by it, should have considerable success in doing this. Grégoire, for example, who comes to Hegel from scholastic thought, is able to make refined comparisons between Hegelian and scholastic relations.[23] This leads him to identify Hegel's *correlative constitutive relation* with the scholastic *transcendental* one,[24] and thus to make a penetrating analysis of the subtle Hegelian use of the cited

---

[19] Hartmann, *Hegel und das Problem der Realdialektik*, Bl. f. d. Phil. 9 (1935/36), p. 5; Coreth, *op. cit.*, pp. 19, 20.
[20] Coreth, *op. cit.*, p. 20.
[21] Findlay, *Hegel*, p. 76 ff.
[22] Aquinas, *Summa Theologiae*, I, 28, 1 in corp. "Ad cuius evidentiam considerandum est quod solum in his quae dicuntur ad aliquid inveniuntur aliqua secundum rationem tantum et non secundum rem . . ."
[23] Coreth, *op. cit.*, p. 24.
[24] *Ibidem*.

relation for structuring being. His conclusions may or may not be valid but they are, at least, an indication of what can be achieved by the more flexible and nuanced scholastic approach.

4. Bradley's Contribution

The extreme defects of too univocal a notion of relation are most clearly manifested in the doctrine of Bradley. He takes the problem of relation as central, and attempts to deal with it critically. It thus dominates his thought. He does not hesitate to admit this nor to admit its difficult consequences. In doing this, he gives a lucid exposition of what exactly is lost in the interpretation of Hegel's doctrine when one does not distinguish the specific *ratios* of relations. This reveals what has brought the modern commentators to an impasse.

B. Bradley's Doctrine on Relation and the Structure of Experience

1. Relation and the Beginning of Experience

a. That the Beginning is *One*

Bradley attempts first to defend the Hegelian doctrine that reality is a relational structure between two extreme poles of *Bare Being* and *Absolute Spirit*. The beginning, according to this, since it is *bare*, is undifferentiated.[25] It is therefore not a multiplicity but a *unity*. Bradley holds this to be the truth.

> Every man's world, the whole world, I mean, in which his self is also included, is one, and it comes to his mind as one universe . . . But this unity is perhaps for the most men no more than an underlying felt whole . . . But none the less the unity is experienced as real.[26]

The world is a felt and unified *whole*. It is a unity experienced as real.[27]

From this it follows that the beginning of experience cannot contain relations.

> In *Mind*, for July 1887, I myself wrote, 'In the beginning there is nothing beyond what is . . . felt simply . . . There are in short no relations and no feelings, only feeling. It is all one blur with differences

---

[25] *Logik* I, Gl. 4, p. 88.
[26] Bradley, *Essays on Truth and Reality*, p. 31.
[27] *Ibidem*.

that work and are felt, but are not discriminated. But of course, following Hegel, I was always clear that this is not the whole of our actual world, and cannot possibly be the end.[28]

Hegel evidently meant this when he asserted in the *Phenomenology of Mind,* that the object of immediate experience is not a grouping of distinct properties (Menge unterschiedener Beschaffenheiten) nor a mutiple relativity to other things (vielfaches Verhalten zu andern).[29] Neither relation nor mediation (Vermittelung) pertain to its nature.[30]

For this reason, Bradley concludes, the beginning of experience is *one* because it is not *relational,* and not *relational* because it is *one.* It is a datum of "feeling" which does not *discriminate,* i.e. does not make relations and therefore contains none. Feeling contains only undifferentiated unity.

If we suppose that this is so, it follows that the beginning excludes relation. For its unity excludes the diverse sides and the oppositions of relations. It is a complete unity, both objectively and subjectively. It makes no discrimination in its object, nor between the subject and the object. It is a "blur".

On this basis Bradley attacks *Associationism.*[31] It is a doctrine which neglects the unity and continuity of the felt background of experience,[32] reducing the latter to a diversity of absolute objects tied together by relations. The unity of original experience is thus destroyed and relations are placed in it where they cannot possible be.[33]

He is so strongly convinced of this for a reason which is not explicitly given in the texts. He is really concerned with rational relations in discourse. This makes his conviction intelligible. For, rational discourse is a concatenation of distinct concepts by the relation of identity.[34] Its absolute point of departure, then, is the unity of reality (unum re) and its plurality and multiplicity is the product of the mind (multa ratione). If we suppose that Bradley has this in mind, then we can understand why he should stress so forcefully the necessity of unity excluding relation in the beginning of experience.

---

[28]*Ibidem,* p. 157, footnote.
[29]*Phänomenologie des Geistes,* Cl. 2, p. 82.
[30]*Ibidem.*
[31]Bradley, *Essays on Truth and Reality,* p. 195.
[32]Bradley, *Appearance and Reality,* p. 107.
[33]*Ibidem.*
[34]Aquinas, *Summa Theologiae,* I, 85, 5, ad 3; I, 13, 12, corp.

The validity of this understanding is confirmed by the fact that the relations which Bradley posits as responsible for subsequently introducing plurality into the original unity are those of position and negation, that is to say, relations of reason which are fundamental in discourse.

He summarizes this doctrine in the following words:

> There is an immediate feeling, a knowing and being in one, with which knowledge begins; and, though this in a manner is transcended, it nevertheless remains throughout as the present foundation of my known world.[35]

b. Against *Pluralism*

1. The Position in Itself: The Beginning is not One

Pluralism has a contrary understanding of experience.

> There is a well-known view that, whatever is given at first, it is not the one Reality; and that hence that One must be reached, if at all, by some supervening process. Our beginning, it is asserted, is with the mere Many.[36]

The beginning then, is *not* one, and if oneness is to belong at any time to experience, this must be after the beginning through some mediating process.

For this point of view Bradley's initial experience is an intellectual *blancmange*.[37] It renders the distinct *confused*. By doing this it may explain the unity of the world (the less obvious aspect) it does away with its diversity (the more obvious aspect).

Russell saw things quite differently from Bradley:

> The world is a world of many things, with relations which are not to be deduced from a supposed nature or scholastic essence of the related things. There is no identity in difference, there is identity and there is difference, and complexes may have some elements identical and some different, but we are no longer obliged to say of any pair of objects that may be mentioned that they are both identical and different.[38]

The ultimate reality of the world is the *many*, not the *one*. Relations do not constitute this *manyness*, but follow upon it. The mind adds

---

[35]Bradley, *Essays on Truth and Reality*, pp. 159, 160.
[36]*Ibidem*, p. 199.
[37]Gellner, *Words and Things*, p. 71.
[38]Bradley, *Essays on Truth and Reality*, pp. 152, 153; Russell, *Philosophical Essays*, p. 169; Bosanquet, *Logic* II, p. 277.

them to it and does not take them from supposed nature or scholastic essence. They are not reducible to simply identity. Nor is differentiation contained within identity. This removes all obligation to hold that diversity *in* identity constitutes the plurality of the world. This contradicts the Hegelian position that diversity presupposes identity, and that whenever we admit the diversity of any "pair of objects" we must also admit their sameness.

Russell holds, on the contrary, that the relations found in experience are "added by the mind".[39] They are the only unity of experience which, therefore, until it is known and judged, is a pure plurality.[40] Believing this to be the case, he seeks to find not the *real essences* of things but their *logical constructions*.

> Whenever possible, logical constructions are to be substituted for inferred entities.[41]

Logical constructions are the real "truth" of experience. In any valid philosophy they should take the place of "supposed essences".

He applies this doctrine not only to the object of experience but also to its subject:

> Why should not the thinker be simply a series of thoughts, connected with each other by a casual law.[42]

If this is the case, then the plurality of the thinker is his "thoughts", and his unity, their connections.

2. Bradley's Reply

Bradley attacks this position by a series of objections. If unity, first of all, is not given at the beginning, it cannot thereafter be achieved. The initial disunity of subject knowing and object known is generally admitted never to result in subsequent unity. Knowledge never transcends it.[43] He himself is of this opinion. This is a sign that initial disunity can never be overcome. Modern thinkers, admitting the truth of this, posit an undifferentiated point of departure in experience. Bradley himself does this under the influence of Hegel.

---

[39]*Ibidem.*
[40]Russell, *Mysticism and Logic,* p. 155.
[41]*Ibidem.*
[42]Russell, *An Outline of Philosophy,* p. 171.
[43]Bradley, *Essays on Truth and Reality,* p. 199.

When it was that the view in question (the unity of initial experience) was first advocated in modern philosophy, I cannot, I regret to say, inform the reader. But that I myself derived it from Hegel is perfectly certain.[44]

A real plurality, again, implies relations and they imply a superior *unity*.

> To suppose the universe plural is therefore to contradict oneself, and, after all, to suppose that it is one. Add one world to another, and forthwith both worlds have become relative, each the finite appearance of a higher and single Reality.[45]

To assert that reality is plural is to qualify it. To qualify is to relate. And what is *related* is opposed and outside. "Plurality" is therefore *outside* of the "real" and thus, the *real* is not itself "plural".[46] To assert the contrary is to fall into contradiction.

The premise of this argument is worth noting. What is relative is opposed. The "plural" is relative to "reality" in the notion of a "plural reality". It is therefore opposed to reality.

In a second argument Bradley attacks so-called "external" relations which, he thinks, are the essence of *Pluralism*. *Pluralism* posits many absolutes existing independently of the mind.[47] The mind takes these into itself by adding relations to them. Such relations do not internally affect the real. They are, for this reason, "external".[48] Bosanquet understands them as a contradiction of Bradley's "internal" relations. External relations are such as are not grounded in the natures of the related things and do not therefore intrinsically affect them.[49] "Internal relations", on the contrary, are so grounded and therefore essentially affect the terms they relate.[50] In support of Bradley, Bosanquet somewhat plaintively criticizes the Pluralists:

> They are extreme absolutists. They are not content to have the Absolute 'in the end', as we more modestly claim it, not meaning after a lapse of time, but in so far as what are fragments for us point out to us a completion beyond them. And there is surely a difference of completeness in different experiences. But they will

---

[44] *Ibidem*, p. 152, 153.
[45] Bradley, *Appearance and Reality*, pp. 519, 520.
[46] *Ibidem*, p. 142.
[47] *Ibidem*, p. 228.
[48] Bradley, *Essays on Truth and Reality*, p. 281.
[49] Bosanquet, *Logic*, II, p. 277.
[50] *Ibidem*.

THE TREATMENT OF THIS DOCTRINE BY LATER PHILOSOPHERS   77

have the Absolute here and now; and to make it handy and adaptable for everyday use they split it into little bits. A universe of tiny Absolutes; that is really what they have to offer us. But if any of these Absolutes imply a term beyond themselves their absolutism breaks down. And we have tried to show that in all relations this is the case.[51]

A plurality, therefore, in immediate experience, is a contradiction. For if its relations are grounded in the natures involved, they fuse into a higher unity, i.e. *not* a plurality. And if they are not so grounded, they demand the same higher unity in order to exist. In either case *Pluralism* is absurd.

Bradley feels that Russell's *Pluralism* at least, is absurd:

> Mr. Russell's main position has remained to myself incomprehensible. On the one side I am let to think that he defends a strict pluralism, for which nothing is admissible beyond simple terms and external relations. On the other side, Mr. Russell seems to assert emphatically, and to use throughout, ideas which such a pluralism surely must repudiate. He throughout stands upon unities which are complex and which cannot be analyzed into terms and relations. These two positions to my mind are irreconcilable, since the second, as I understand it, contradicts the first flatly.[52]

Russell holds for "unities" and this means for "internal relations" but at the same time he posits a strict pluralism, and this means purely "external relations". The possibility of these purely "external" relations is the crucial point.

3. The Crucial Point: External Relations

The possibility of "external relations" is essential to the Pluralist position. Without them, it collapses. Bradley tries to show that they are absurd.

He notes, first of all, an awkward consequence which follows from positing them. They do not affect an object intrinsically but are added to it from without. If this is the case, why can they not be added in any way whatsoever? Why cannot "before" be attributed to the cart rather than to the horse and why should "putting the cart before the horse" be generally considered ridiculous? By extension, why cannot the order of relations be changed everywhere in reality?[53] The fact that we

---

[51]*Ibidem*, pp. 279, 280.
[52]Bradley, *Essays on Truth and Reality*, p. 281.
[53]*Ibidem*, pp. 292, 293, 294.

would think this strange indicates that relations are not as external to their terms as Russell would have us believe.

The position, moreover, that there are such things as external relations implies that they can be separated from their terms and even considered by the mind without being applied. Bradley tries to show that this is untenable.

> Is it possible to think of a relation as being real apart from all terms? I understand that Mr. Russell affirms this possibility, and further adduces arguments in favor of its existence in fact.[54]

But this is impossible, as direct experiment proves.[55]

> The method actually followed may be called in the main the procedure used by Hegel, that of a direct ideal experiment made on reality.[56]

It consists in positing a relation and then trying to think away its terms. The effort fails. Therefore, Bradley concludes, the attempt is absurd and "termless" relations are impossible. But these are the same as "external" relations. "External relations", therefore, are impossible.

> To have bare A in bare external relation to B is not possible in any observation or experiment . . . There is always here a condition left outside of what you take as the fact . . . To say something about A which in no sense qualifies A, remains to my mind meaningless. In other words, no 'and' which is purely external is thinkable.[57]

The same argument is repeated in other texts. Relations, if they are held to exist, must *qualify* the *world*. But in this case, "external" relations would have to qualify the sole intelligible world externally. This is self-contradicting and meaningless.[58]

> There is no identity or likeness except in a whole, and every such whole must qualify and be qualified by its terms.[59]

Russell's argument from "analysis", moreover, which supposedly shows that there are such things as "external" relations, is likewise fallacious.

> Mr. Russell urges, as I understand, that the fact of analysis proves the existence of bare relations. For, if you were not acquainted with

---

[54] *Ibidem.*
[55] *Ibidem,* p. 311.
[56] *Ibidem.*
[57] *Ibidem,* p. 290.
[58] *Ibidem.*
[59] Bradley, *Appearance and Reality,* p. 579.

THE TREATMENT OF THIS DOCTRINE BY LATER PHILOSOPHERS 79

these relations by themselves, the result of the analysis would to you be meaningless.[60]

Analysis only reveals the parts in a complex whole. It does not give them intelligibility. That they are already supposed to have. Analysis simply discovers that these previously understood contents exist for a fact in that whole. They are themselves, therefore, intelligible without their terms. This proves that *termless* relations exist.

Bradley denies this by the method of a direct experiment on reality. Is it possible mentally to conceive of these relations without some terms? If it is not, and clearly this is the case, then Russell's argument is invalid.[61] Termless relations cannot even be conceived let alone exist.

Comparison seems to demonstrate the contrary.[62] Things, which are compared, are not actually related until the mind compares them. The comparison is thus external to them (i.e. it is something outside of them in the comparing mind). Bradley counters by asking: Does the comparison attain the truth of things? If it does, then how can the relation which it makes be said to "fall outside of its terms"?[63]

A famous argument is taken from the problem of *constructing series*. Obviously a finite series, if it could be constructed with purely external relations, would show that the latter are possible. Russell proposes to do this and thereby to set Bradley's "holism" aside.[64] Bradley tries to show that the attempt is an illusion.

> Given a plurality of terms, and given one relation of a certain sort, to be taken in as many instances as you please—and I agree that with this you can make a series. But I deny emphatically that the series is really made out of nothing more . . . From the terms and the relation, as materials, the series cannot be made *anyhow*, and the question as to the how to myself seems vital.[65]

For the "how" is the "end" and this is not *external* to the series since it is *immanent* in it. The "end" is that factor of a series which is always identical, of which each member is a part, and aside from which the series has no meaning, sense or direction.[66]

---

[60]Bradley, *Essays on Truth and Reality*, p. 299.
[61]*Ibidem*.
[62]Bradley, *Appearance and Reality*, p. 578.
[63]*Ibidem*.
[64]Bradley, *Essays on Truth and Reality*, p. 308.
[65]*Ibidem*, p. 308, 309.
[66]*Ibidem*.

Arguing in this trenchant fashion Bradley is convinced that he has set aside every possible objection to the unity of the beginning of experience.

c. Summary

In sum, he argues to the unity of initial experience in two different ways:

1. if the beginning is not *one*, then unity will never subsequently be reached;
2. if it is not *one*, then all its relations will be external and, therefore, self-contradicting.

From this he concludes that the beginning of experience cannot be relational, since it is *one* and relation, being essentially an opposition of terms, is not.

d. Criticism

Bradley's argument depends upon an undifferentiated notion of relation as a sort of opposition. The one cannot contain this without losing its unity. A deeper insight into types of relation would show this conclusion to be false. The Aristotalian relation of "proportional" or "analogous unity" would not support it. Bradley's argument may therefore be said to conclude to *some* sort of unity in being, whose negation would truly lead to intelligible chaos in scepticism, such a *Pluralism* is hard put to avoid. But it cannot be held to conclude to an *absolute* unity. Russell's arguments against it are, in this respect fully justified. Bradley is a latter day Parmenides, positing univocity of being. He cannot, therefore, any more than the Greek philosopher explain the patent diversity of reality. To this extent his doctrine unrealistic.[67]

Its lucid reasonings are not, however, without value. They have great value in that they place the burden of acquiring a deeper insight in relation upon the shoulders of anyone who wishes to avoid Bradley unrealism. They show up the results of an inadequate insight. Bradley may not be right, yet to prove this one must dig deeper into the doctrine of relation.

Heidegger's intuition is sure when he says, at the beginning "Sein und Zeit", that the fundamental problem of philosophy is th

---

[67] Gellner, *Words and Things*, pp. 71, 72.

THE TREATMENT OF THIS DOCTRINE BY LATER PHILOSOPHERS 81

of being and that its profoundest solution up to now is Aristotle's doctrine of analogy.[68]

2. Relation and the Transcendence of Immediate Experience

Bradley is convinced by Hegel, then, that the beginning of experience is undifferentiated being. He is also convinced by the same philosopher that this is not its end.

> But of course, following Hegel, I was always clear taht this beginning is not the whole of our actual world, and cannot possibly be the end.[69]

There is something beyond immediate experience which transcends it. And the principle, by which this transcendancy is achieved, is *relation*.[70] For the transcending content conflicts with immediate experience, i.e. *relates* to it.

> Everything that is real must be felt. But, on the other side, I urge that our felt content is developed in such a way that it goes beyond and conflicts with the form of feeling or immediacy.[71]

What is real is an object of immediate experience in feeling where there is no objective or subjective differentiation.[72] Plurality is *beyond* this. In order to be "real", then, it must be in some way *in* the latter. This can only be through *relation*. Relation, then, is the principle of transcendence and of the "plural reality".

a. Relation as Effecting the Transcendence

Through relation plurality adheres to reality without destroying its unity. As an "opposition" or a "conflict" it stands *over against* unity. *As to* reality, it is identical with it. This Bradley calls "ideality" making it thus clear that he has in mind such relations as constitute the ideal. These he places outside of the real. James understands this to mean that the relations are not real. Although their terms are. This is erroneous. Bradley does not mean this at all. For him *both* terms and relation are *alike unreal* and both are outside of the real as opposed to it. Both are *abstractions*.[73]

---

[68]Heidegger, *Sein und Zeit*, Volume I, Chapter I.
[69]Bradley, *Essays on Truth and Reality*, p. 157 footnote 1.
[70]*Ibidem*, p. 160.
[71]*Ibidem*, p. 157.
[72]*Ibidem*, p. 199.
[73]Bradley, *Essays on Truth and Reality*, p. 151, footnote 1.

Relation, then, added to the unity of experience produces a "higher Reality" transcendsing the immediate immersion in being. But, as being *to* immediacy, this transcending content includes it. It is *negation*, therefore, but also *identity*.[74] In it the felt content of immediate experience developes into the "object which satisfies me".[75] The latter can be accounted for only in this way.

Bradley therefore agrees with Hegel not only regarding the unity of immediate experience, but also regarding the function of relations in the structuring of the categories. These objects of mediated experience are created through the implanting of relations in the original unity of being. And thereby "my object is increased" by an addition to that "which was and is felt" whose result is a "positive sense of expansion and of accord". This is not only a *negation* within *identity*, but also a *position*. Thus it is an "accord".[76]

Relation, in this way, solves the problem of unity and multiplicity in experience. It transforms an original immediate and unified experience into an object, i.e. into opposition to a subject.

> The solution, if I may anticipate, is in general supplied by considering the fact, that immediate experience, however much transecnded both remains and is active. It is not a stage which shows itself at the beginning and then disappears, but it remains at the bottom throughout as fundamental.[77]

In this evolution, immediate experience remains as that which receives and supports the relations whereby it is transcended, so that it is always present in higher experience.

The beginning and end are one; multiplicity lies in between. Thus contradiction is found neither in Being nor in Absolute Knowledge but in mediating multiplicity.

> Contradiction in the proper sense thus belongs to the middle space of our reflective world, and it may be said to inhabit that region, or rather part of that region, which lies between feeling and perfect experience.[78]

Relation thus explains the categories, just as Hegel taught, and first of all, that of Quality.

[74]*Ibidem.*
[75]*Ibidem*, p. 171.
[76]*Ibidem.*
[77]*Ibidem*, pp. 160, 161.
[78]*Ibidem*, p. 271.

THE TREATMENT OF THIS DOCTRINE BY LATER PHILOSOPHERS 83

> Qualities are nothing without relations ... To define qualities without relations is surely impossible. In the field of consciousness, even when we abstract from the relations of identity and difference, they are never independent.[79]

One cannot conceive of quality without conceiving of relation. Relation, therefore, essentially constitutes the plurality which is Quality. It also constitutes the category of *Appearance*.

> Everything which appears must be predicated of Reality but it must not be predicted in such a way as to make Reality contradict itself.[80]

Appearance is through "predication of Reality" and therefore through the relation of qualification. Without this relation, then, it cannot exist. Bradley, in asserting this, is not concerned with the special Hegelian category of *relation*, but with *identity, negation* and *position*.

Much the same doctrine is taught by McTaggart:

> I hold that the existence of qualities involves the existence of Substances. I should define a substance as that which has qualities and *is related*, without being itself either a quality or a relation, or having quailties or relations among its parts.[81]

A quality *is* in relation to a subject, and without this relation, it is nothing. But, at the same time, since it is related to a subject, it is also opposed to it, and therefore not *in* it. This is also true of relation. And therefore substance *has* qualities and is *related*, but *is not* itself a quality or a relation.

Royce, on the basis of the existence of error, arrives at the same conclusion.[82] But the difficulties of the argument make him hestitate to believe it fully. For this reason he does not want to be called a pure Hegelian. He is more a disciple of Peirce, the "unduly neglected American logician", than either an idealist or a follower of Hegel.[83]

b. Difficulties of the Position

Royce hestitated to assert that the introduction of *identity* and *diverity* into the initial absolute unity of being gives an adequate explan-

---

[79]Bradley, *Appearance and Reality*, p. 26.
[80]Bradley, *Essays on Truth and Reality*, p. 224.
[81]McTaggart, *Philosophical Studies*, p. 275.
[82]Werkmeister, *A History of Philosophical Ideas in America*, pp. 134, 135.
[83]*Ibidem*, p. 133.

ation of its observed multiplicity. It seems rather to make multiplicity a fiction and relations unreal. This consideration triggered off a strong reaction to Bradley's "holism", in spite of that philosopher's great authority. Logical Atomism thus arose as the expression of a common rejection of Bradley's "unrealistic picture of the world".[84] It was a denial of his "quasi-logical doctrine of the unreality of relations".[85]

The doctrine of Bradley, therefore, gives rise to two difficulties:

1. it makes the distinction of the *many* in reality an illusion;
2. it makes relation unreal.

His too generic concept of relation is responsible for this. He holds it to be an undifferentiated "opposition" whose presence excludes unity. For this reason he makes plurality and relation itself *not real*. The conclusions are logical but, for the majority of thinkers, unacceptable since they seem not to correspond to the world of experience.

c. Criticism

The truth, in this particular problem, seems partially to be found on both sides. Bradley is justified in asserting that plurality involves relation. But he is wrong in holding that any relation whatsoever is *excluded* from unified being, or that plurality *is not* real. The Thomistic doctrine of the proportional unity of being makes reality truly both one and many.

Those who opposed Bradley as unrealistic were therefore justified in doing so. But they were not able to offer an adequate theoretical grounding for their conviction. And thus they made as serious a mistake as Bradley in their *exclusion* of *unity* from the "initial experience." They lacked the broader and more nuanced notion of relation and its various types which would have reconciled their conflicting opinions.

3. Relation and the Termination of Experience in the Absolute

Bradley presents the case for relation with the greatest clarity, both in his principles of judgment and in his conclusions, in dealing with the Absolute.

---

[84] Gellner, *Words and Things*, p. 71.
[85] *Ibidem*, p. 72.

a. No Relation in the Absolute

The "ultimate reality", he asserts:

> ... is not a mere aspect or aspects, but it is a unity in which every distinction is at once maintained and subordinated.[86]

It is not a "mere aspect" since, if it were, then it would be a "side" or a "view from a side". This could not be ultimate. Other such views would always lie beside or beyond it. The ultimate must be such as to exclude anything beside or beyond it. It cannot, therefore, be an aspect. And since an aspect is relative, the ultimate cannot be this. It is a relationless oneness.

Its unity is not, however, the same as that of immediate experience. Immediate experience is a oneness *before* plurality, and thus excluding it. Ultimate experience is a oneness *after* plurality, and thus transcending and subsuming it. Ultimate experience *maintains* and *subordinates* plurality, preserving it, in Hegel's sense.[87] The ultimate maintains and subordinates all distinction.

For this reason,

> Reality . . . is a higher unity above our immediate experience, and above all ideality and relations. It is above thought and will and aesthetic perception. But, though transcending these modes of experience, it includes them fully.[88]

Things in the plural world exist by their opposition one to the other, but above all by their opposition to the ultimate. They can only exist in so far as they are "maintained" by this last relationship. The ultimate, however, is not relative to them. It neither contains relation within itself nor has relation to anything outside of itself. In the end, "the absolute is related to nothing . . ."[89]

It is thus above "ideality and relations". But thought, and will and aesthetic perception are ideational and relational. Therefore the Absolute is above these too. It is not a *self* which *wills* and *thinks*.

> Will in my judgement must imply something in the self or beyond the self which is other than will, and, apart from this 'other', I cannot find any sense or meaning in the will either of man or of God. There

---

[86] Bradley, *Essays on Truth and Reality*, p. 75.
[87] *Logik* I, Cl. 4, p. 120.
[88] Bradley, *Essays on Truth and Reality*, p. 343.
[89] *Ibidem*, p. 427.

is to me no thinking without something which thinks and again something which is thought of—something in either case which is other than mere thought.[90]

The Absolute, cannot be conceived of in terms of the ancient quarrel over the primacy of intellect or will. It is not even the *identity* of the two.[91]

Does this Absolute correspond to the traditional God of Will and Intellect?

> I have not, I know, to repeat to those who are acquainted with my book that for me the Absolute is not God. God for me has no meaning outside of the religious consciousness, and that essentially is practical. The Absolute for me cannot be God, because in the end the Absolute is related to nothing, and there cannot be a practical relation between it and the finite will.[92]

The argument is clear and categorical. Relation *is* opposition. There is no opposition in the Absolute. The Absolute contains no relations. But "willing" and "thinking" are relations. Therefore they are not in the Absolute. In this same context St. Thomas distinguishes the relation of creatures to God, which is real, from the inverse relation of God to creatures, which is a product of reason.[93] And he casts a profound light upon the problem of intelligence and volition in God by His notion of *how* they are relational.

> ... a personal God is not the ultimate truth about the Universe, and in that ultimate truth would be included and superseded by something higher than personality. A God that can say to himself 'I' as against you and me, is not in my judgement defensible as the last and complete truth for metaphysics.[94]

b. The Heart of the Argument

Bradley argues, in this way, from a generic notion of relation neglecting its specific types. To this he attributes an inner opposition which excludes unity and is incompatible with the Absolute.

The Absolute has neither *knowledge* nor *will* since these, too, imply relation. It is therefore *not* a person. This agrees with Neoplato-

[90] *Ibidem*, pp. 96, 192 ff.
[91] Bradley, *Appearance and Reality*, p. 476, 477.
[92] Bradley, *Essays on Truth and Reality*, p. 427.
[93] Aquinas, *Summa Theologiae*, I, 45, 3, ad 1.
[94] Bradley, *Essays on Truth and Reality*, p. 432.

metaphysics to the extent that Nous is placed outside of the One, since it involves knowledge and therefore distinction. Bradley cannot conceive of a higher mode of being in which that which is really opposed in lower forms of knowledge should be identical. His insistence upon the use of an undifferentiated notion of relation makes this inconceivable for him.

c. Objection Against It

McTaggart criticizes Bradley for his notion of self-consciousness:

> Of those philosophies which, without falling into complete scepticism, deny the reality of the self, the two important ones are Hume's and Bradley's . . . (Bradley) . . . points out that most, if not all, of the content of the self can become an object, and from this he concludes that very little, if any, of the content of the self can belong to it essentially. His view is that what becomes an object becomes *ipso facto* part of the non-self, and what is non-self cannot be the self or part of it. If Bradley is right in holding that whatever becomes an object must be removed from the self, then it is clear that no self can know its own existence.[95]

This text is particularly interesting. McTaggart accepts the principle that relation makes knowledge in the Absolute impossible. For knowledge *is* relation; relation *is* opposition; and opposition is exclusion. To the extent that the self knows itself, it is opposed to itself, and therefore outside itself. This calls for an attack upon its premises, and a distinction between types of relation. McTaggart is obviously unable to make this move. He contents himself with checking the premises through the conclusion. Does the self in fact know its own existence? Of course it does. Bradley's position is unrealistic and therefore wrong. His argument is weak because it does not come to grips with the real problem: how can Bradley be wrong, granting that his notion of relation is adequate? Before the problem McTaggart hesitates: "If Bradley is right in holding that whatever becomes an object must be removed from the self . . ."

It is clear, then, that Bradley's reasoning is more consistent and his principles more evident. He cannot be criticized for failing to clarify Hegel's thought. Hegel is just as defective as he. Hegel posited Nous and relation in the structure of the categories but he did not know how these are theoretically possible.

[95] McTaggart, *Philosophical Studies*, pp. 81, 82.

Grégoire, in his third Étude, shows the confusion to which this has led.[96] He enumerates five distinct interpretations of the Absolute Idea. They are divided into two main classes:

1. Those which hold that the Absolute is self-conscious;
2. Those which hold that it is not.

The author, due to his scholastic background, has no difficulty in dealing with either. This is not Bradley's case. One may well hesitate to affirm that it was Hegel's. If it was, then his obscure expression is puzzling.

On this point Royce, too, opposes Bradley. He thinks that Hegel has established the contrary thesis by proving three propositions:

1. that thought and being are identical;
2. that the categories are reducible to thought;
3. that the dialectical method is universally applicable.

Thought, by the first, is *in* being, just as being is *in* thought. The second proposition shows that Absolute Self-consciousness connects with the categories. The third proves the same point pragmatically. Since it works, it thereby establishes its own validity.[97]

This, however, is not so simply conclusive. Hegel offers no theoretical justification for identifying thought with being. He simply posits this. As a result, he does not show us how to get around Bradley. the Absolute is self-conscious, then Bradley is wrong. But how can it be when this implies relation which the Absolute excludes? Neither Hegel nor Royce gives us the answer.

C. Summary and Criticism

1. Summary

The Absolute which comes after plurality is, for Bradley, then, on From this he concludes that it excludes relations. He concludes that because he conceives of relation as involving opposition and limitation. As a consequence, he denies that the Absolute is self-conscious, i.e. has intelligence, will or personality. It transcends all three.

[96] Grégoire, *Études Hégéliennes*, p. 140 ff.
[97] Royce, *Lectures on Modern Idealism*, p. 230.

2. Criticism

The root of this argument is an undifferentiated notion of relation. Relation is conceived without qualification as limiting opposition. It is therefore excluded from the Absolute. But this is invalid. The reaction of ordinary common sense manifests as much. And philosophical insight into relation, taken in the abstract, shows that this posits nothing as to the reality or the unreality of its terms, and transcends the distinction of the "real" and the "rational". Thus it may or may not involve real distinction and limitation. In rational knowledge, it involves both. In the self-consciousness of the Absolute, it involves neither.[98] Distinction, here, is all-important. Without distinction, reasoning is inconclusive. The absolute cannot have a real relation of dependence, of course, or real intrinsic relations of composition. But it does not follow from this that all relationality is excluded from it, and that the Absolute therefore has neither knowledge or will. It has both but not through a relation involving real limitation. It has them through the relation of identity.[99] The subtle scholastic doctrine of intentionality brings this out. Bradley's less subtle doctrine limits the possibilities of his thought.

But one cannot say that Bradley, in this matter, has misunderstood Hegel. Misunderstood is not the word. He has attempted to give precise theoretical grounding to Hegel's ambiguous doctrine. But although, in this, he has failed, the attempt still has value. It points the way to making sense out of Hegel's dialectic. Only a more refined and flexible doctrine of relation will do this.

---

[98] Aquinas, *Summa Theologiae*, I, 14, 2 corp.
[99] *Ibidem*.

CHAPTER VI

SUMMARY AND CRITICISM

Relation, there can be no doubt, is one of the most difficult studies in all of philosophy. Modern scholastics, impressed by this fact, like to quote the words of Dominicus Flandricus:

> Since relation is the lowest form of being and consequently has the least intelligibility . . . it is not surprising that there should be a difference of opinion concerning it . . . It is a difficult and ambiguous matter in the extreme . . . Whether anyone who mentions it understands what he is talking about, I don't know. God knows.[1]

Aristotle, without the rhetoric, affirms the same obscurity of this subject.[2] There can be no doubt that it is obscure in itself, and, for this reason, it is no surprise that it should be obscure in Hegel. He does not relieve the situation. He makes much of relation, employing it everywhere in the structuring of being and thought. But he nowhere teaches us precisely what it is. He seems to attach no particular significance to its various forms in the structure of his system.

Yet, reflection upon his way of using it permits us to make certain systematization. From this, it is possible to form an Hegelian doctrine on relation as a whole; to interpret the special relation of "reconciliation"; and, finally, to evaluate Hegel's contribution of this subject to all of modern philosophy.

A. Summary of the Hegelian Doctrine on Relation

Hegel applies the name "relation" to three broad domains: the Category of Relation properly so-called; to that of Quantitative and Absolute Relation; and to what he calls "reference" (Beziehung

---

[1]Dominicus Flandricus, *In Meta. Arist. Lib.* V, q. 16, a. 18.
[2]Aristotle, *Categories*, VIII, 8 a 29 ff.

1. The Category of Relation

The category of relation he defines as a "determined mode of appearance." He thus makes it correlative to appearance as its "totally universal mode." This means, he explains, that it must contain all things that exist. By this condition it is correlative to existence.[3] At least this applies to "essential relationship", which, of its nature, is immediately involved in the structure of appearance and of existence.

The *category* of relation is therefore that of Essential Relation. As such it is a structural principle in Appearance. Everything which appears does so through its presence. And since everything which exists *appears*, this relation is everywhere.

Now, Appearance is always Appearance of parts in the unity of a whole. This, therefore, is the first Essential Relation. It is static and must give place to the dynamic. It therefore yields to a second Essential Relation, that of *Force* and *Manifestation*. This, in the last analysis, gives rise to a relation of *Inner* to *Outer*. In this way the third Essential Relation arises.[4]

2. Other Relations

Essential relation is found in the category of Appearance. But before it, in the category of Quantity, there is Quantitative Relation (quantitative Verhältniss) and after it, in the category of Actuality, there is Absolute Relation. The former is distinguished from Essential Relation in that its terms are not totalities; the latter by the fact that its terms fuse into *one*. The Inner becomes the Outer and relation itself dissolves (geht zu Grunde).[5]

3. Reference (Beziehung)

But these relations do not exhaust the possibilities of the genus. There is still another type. It is the more radical and fundamental relation of *Beziehung* or "reference."[6] This basic relation has three movements:

---

[3] Encyclopädie, Gl. 6, p. 80.
[4] Text, Chapter I.
[5] Text, Chapter I.
[6] Text, Chapter IV.

1. position;
2. negation;
3. reconciliation.⁷

Every content of reality and of thought is structured by these. They give Hegel's thought its richness and synthetic unity. It is not possible to treat them as if they shared the same *ratio* as the category of Relation. "Verhältniss" and "Beziehung" have something in common, but much that is different. The difference must be stressed.

Hegel indicates as much by the fact that he never speaks of "relation as such", as Bradley does, but always of particular types. He speaks always of Negation, Force and Manifestation, and so on. And he is careful to distinguish Quantitative Relation from Essential Relation and to tell us that we may apply Negation immediately to being but not Ground and Consequence (Grund und Folge).⁸

Yet he has no organic doctrine in which the implications of these distinctions are made explicit. Nowhere does he show us exactly how the *ratio* of relation is found in Position, Negation and Reconciliation as opposed to the way in which it is found in Quantitative Ratio or in Essential and Absolute Relation.

As a result his commentators, lacking themselves a nuanced doctrine by which to judge, cannot make complete sense of the system. Hartmann looks upon it as a piecemeal work (Detailarbeit) lacking unity.⁹ Hegel himself, he is convinced, saw no genuine unity in it and had no clear consciousness of a method (klares Methodenbewusstsein).¹⁰ Coreth thinks this opinion extreme but he does admit a discrepancy between Hegel's conception of his method, and his application of it. In principle, the method is unambiguous (eindeutig), but not in application. The numerous changes which it undergoes in the *Logic* and the *Encyclopedia* are extensive (weitgreifende) and profound (tiefgreifende).¹¹ Hegel allows its particular matter to dominate it.¹² But he still maintains a certain formal structure (eine gewisse formale Struktur) in every case and this is its "unity".¹³

---

⁷*Ibidem.*
⁸*Logik* I, Gl. 4, pp. 115, 116.
⁹Hartmann, *op. cit.* p. 5.
¹⁰*Ibidem.*
¹¹Coreth, *op. cit.* p. 21.
¹²*Ibidem.*
¹³*Ibidem.*

It is possible to reconcile this view with the former by positing that the unity of the dialectic is not univocal but analogous. This position, however, must be imposed upon Hegel rather than taken from him. Even so, it has the advantage of making possible a certain systematization of the doctrine without distorting it.

B. Systematization of the Doctrine

1. Abstract Ratio of Relation

The generic *ratio* of Hegelian relation is that of "reference". Hegel posits this in his use of the term *Beziehung*, which signifies a general habitude of one thing to another.

2. Specific *Ratios of Relation*

a. Primary Relation (Beziehung)

Beziehung, however, is not only generic for Hegel; it is also primary. It can be applied immediately to Bare Being and, through this, to the entire structure of reality. It is thus the cause of the secondary relations.

b. Secondary Relations

The secondary relations are not applicable to all of being but only to particular categories. Hegel calls them always *Verhältnisse* rather than *Beziehungen*. He holds that they are found most properly in Essential Relations and least properly in Quantitative and Absolute Relations.

C. Identification of These Relations in a Scholastic Context

A scholastic can identify and systematize all of these Hegelian relations, as Grégoine has partly done,[14] that is the justification of the following attempt.

1. Rational Relations

The primary relations in the Hegelian system which are applied immediately to Bare Being and, then, mediately to the entire system are, from a scholastic point of view, *relations of reason*. *Affirmation* and *negation* are formally found only in the mind, although they

---

[14]Grégoire, *Études Hégéliennes*, p. 73 ff.

have a cause in external reality.[15] They are relations which follow upon things as they are thought and not as they are in reality. They are thus not real structuring principles.

2. Real Relations

The secondary relations are *real*. They are of two types: some are "predicamental" and some, "transcendental."

a. Predicamental Relation

Predicamental relations in scholastic doctrine, are accidents following upon substance and founded on *quality, action* and *passion*.[16] They can easily be identified in the Hegelian scheme.

The Quantitative Relation of *Ratio* is obviously one. Hegel conceives this, however, quite differently from the scholastic. He takes quantity as it is found in judgment and not as in real substances. For this reason, he places it *after* Quality whereas, in scholastic thought, it comes *before*, being its real ground in reality. He thus has not a little difficulty in interpreting it, since he attributes to it real properties in terms of rational relations. This difficulty occurs later again in his interpretation of Reconciliation.

The Essential Relation of Whole and the Part is similar to a scholastic predicamental relation founded upon quantity. Its connection is *mechanical* rather than *dynamic*.[17] It is accidental and extrinsic to the parts, rather than intrinsic to them.

The relations of Causality and Mutual Interaction are likewise from a scholastic point of view, predicamental relations founded on *action and passion*.

b. Transcendental Relation

The transcendental relation in scholastic thought is of the nature of the related thing and not added as an accident. It is the sort of relation which binds accidents to their substances, and act to potency. It, too, can be identified in the Hegelian scheme. Force and its Manifestation involve such a relation. So does the Hegelian relation of Inner and Outer, and that of Substance and Accident in the category of Absolute Relation.

---

[15] Aquinas, *Summa Theologiae*, I, 85, 5, ad 3.
[16] Aristotle, Metaphysics, V, 15, 1020 b 26 ff.
[17] *Logik* I, Cl. 4, p. 648.

3. Mixed Relations

Rational and real relations are mixed together everywhere in Hegel's thought, but nowhere more distressingly than in the relation of Reconciliation (Aufgehobenheit). In so far as this is conceived in the context of the *per se* and the *per participationem* (of the Nous and dependent things) it involves *transcendental real* relations. In so far as it is conceived in the context of affirmations and negations, it involves *rational relations*. That Hegel conceives of it in the first context is clear from his reference to it as a "return into self" (Zurückgehen in sich), i.e. as the self-consciousness of the Nous. That he conceives of it also in the context of rational relations is clear from his definition of it as a "negation of a negation."[18] It is thus a mixture of the rational and the real.

Schema

The doctrine as a whole may be clarified by the following schema. Hegel

Primary Relations (Beziehungen)

Position	rational relation
Negation	rational relation
Reconciliation	mixture of rational and real

Secondary Relations (Verhältnisse)

Quantitative	real predicamental relation
Essential	
Whole — Part	real predicamental relation
Force	real transcendental relation
Inner — Outer	real transcendental relation
Absolute	
Substance	real transcendental relation
Cause	real predicamental relation
Interaction	real predicamental relation

[18] *Philosophie Der Religion*, Gl. 15, p. 451.

Scholastic Doctrine

Rational Relations

Position
Negation

Real Relations

Predicamental

Quantitative Relation
Essential Relation
    Whole and Part

Absolute Relation
    Cause and Effect
    Mutual Interaction

Transcendental

Essential Relation
    Force and its Manifestation
    Inner and Outer

Absolute Relation
    Substance and Accident

Mixed Relation

Reconciliation

Thus the basic division of relation, for the scholastic, is into the rational and the real. For Hegel, it is into primary and secondary. The distinction of the "real" and the "rational" does not exist for him as it does for the scholastic. And thus his doctrine may equally well be considered as "realism" or idealism."[19]

The scholastic must reject the mixture of the "rational" and the "real" in the relation of Reconciliation as totally unacceptable. Hegel considers it crucial. But he nowhere gives this position the sort of treatment which it demands. He nowhere shows us how the combination is possible.

[19]Kuiper, Le "*Réalisme de Hegel*".

D. Difficulty of the Hegelian Doctrine

The chief defect of Hegel's doctrine, then, from the point of view of its formal completeness, is its lack of a well-developed theory of relation. Relation is used throughout as a fundamental structuring principle. But it is never treated with the theoretical precision which this requires. As a result the commentators have an extremely difficult time in interpreting its meaning. This is made lucidly clear in the objections of Bradley for which there is no formal Hegelian answer. The Absolute, Bradley asserts, cannot *know* because knowledge is a *relation* and relation cannot be *in* the Absolute. No argument to the contrary can be found in Hegel's text. And yet, for its completeness, it should contain this. The fact that it does not creates the suspicion that there may be something to Hartmann's doubt that Hegel had a clear consciousness of a method.[20] His mental picture of it must surely have been imprecise.

Findlay feels that this is the case for the relation of negation. Hegel holds that this is the same "reference" which connects Being with Nothing, and Force-Manifestation with Whole-Part. But his identification of these two is difficult to see. The unity of "negation" is obscure.[21]

Ambiguity is likewise found in Reconciliation. For Hegel, this is sometimes simply *one* of *many possible* principles of unity.[22] As such, it differs greatly in the various triads. Its unity thus becomes that of a work of art.

> His dialectical triads certainly reveal a community of style, but this community breaks up, on examination, into a number of distinct resemblances all of which are not present in every case.[23]

This, Findlay thinks, is of the nature of Hegel's doctrine, which excludes mathematical rigor and depends upon "illumination".[24] In substance it is not a rational doctrine but a "mystical insight".

The result of this is that the commentators are unable to give Hegel a precise meaning. They divide on the questions of knowledge in the Absolute, or *contradiction* in the most formal sense as con-

---

[20]Hartmann, *op. cit.*, p. 6 ff.
[21]Findlay, *Hegel*, p. 72.
[22]*Ibidem*, p. 73.
[23]*Ibidem*, p. 74.
[24]*Ibidem*.

stituting being. This makes Hegel a special problem of interpretation. His thought is singularly dense, so that criticisms of his "principles" commonly bog down in attempts to determine just what they are.

This is notoriously the case for the relation of Reconciliation. Of all Hegel's doctrines, this has caused the greatest confusion and difficulty. It can hardly be *criticized* until both are removed.

E. Tentative Interpretation of the Relation of "Reconciliation"

We have already proposed one interpretation of this notion with a view to making intelligible the properties which Hegel attributes to it.[25] Reconciliation may be conceived as formally identical with the relation which holds between the *per se* and the *per participationem* in traditional doctrine. Once this is posed, it immediately explains the Helegian properties of

1. "true infinity" and
2. "resolution of contradiction".[26]

The attempt to justify these on some other ground, such as on the analysis of "position" and "negation", is unsuccessful.[27] There is, moreover, Hegel's positive identification of his sources as Aristotle and the Neoplatonic tradition.[28] The excerpt from the Metaphysics which he places at the end of the end of the *Encyclopedia*, as a sort of summation of his own thought, is particularly significant.[29]

F. Criticism

The relation of Reconciliation is then an amalgam of the traditional relations constitutive of "participating thing" and relations of reason. The first element gives it the appearance of being mystical, and draws down upon it the censure of Hartmann. It is an intuition similar to that of Anaxagoras in positing *Nous*, thereby becoming, in the words of Aristotle, so frequently quoted by Hegel, "like a sober man

[25] *Text*, Chapter IV
[26] *Ibidem*.
[27] *Ibidem*.
[28] Findlay, *Hegel*, p. 64 ff.
[29] *Encyclopädie*, Gl. 10, pp. 475, 476.

among drunks".[30] But, like that of Anaxagoras, it is a defective intuition because it is imprecise. The difficulties which the commentators have had in interpreting it make this clear. Such is the first criticism which can be leveled against it, and all of Hegel's doctrine.

A second is this: that Hegel attempts to unite two orders of relations which are incompatible: the real and the rational. He tries to combine the real relations constituting participation, with those of *position* and *negation*. This cannot be done. Nevertheless it is not difficult to see why he should have made the attempt. He saw that, in the last analysis, and contrary to Bradley, there can be no insurmountable barrier between knowledge and reality. Indeed, the relations which pertain to the creature in so far as he is *thought of* by God, are those which *constitute* his *being*. To be *known*, for him, is *to be*. But this is not true of the relations which pertain to a thing only *in so far* as it is *thought by the human mind,* such as those of "position" and "negation", which have a foundation in reality, but are formally only in reason. These do not constitute the real being of things.

Thus, "to participate" pertains to the real structure of things; to be "affirmed" or "denied", to their rational structure. And though the two orders are interconnected, they are not identically the same. "Affirmation" and "negation" are not identical with the relations which constitute *participation*.

A third and final criticism is this. Hegel assumes that knowledge of the *existence* of a relation is equivalent to *full* knowledge of its *intelligibility*. Thus he supposes that when he can determine the order of "existence" to "essence" he completely understands both. This convinces him that he totally grasps the relationality of "existence" and that the latter is totally rational. A more sophisticated doctrine of relation would have made him hesitate to accept this extreme position which Schelling later attacked.[31]

This is not, however, completely to depreciate Hegel's work. It still has the great merit of reintroducing into modern thought a profound insight of antiquity into the function of Intelligence in the structure

---

[30]Chapter Four, footnote no. 66
[31]Rollo May, *Existence*, p. 15, footnote.

of the world. If this insight is not worked out with precision in the *Logic* and in the *Encyclopedia,* it is nevertheless shown to be fundamental. In the long run, this cannot help but be of benefit. If nothing else, it will force the modern mind to think more deeply into the elusive problem of relation.

BIBLIOGRAPHY

Baillie, J. B., *Hegel's Phenomenology of Mind*. Translation, Introduction and Notes. George Allen & Unwin Ltd. London, 1955.

Bosanquet, Bernard, *Logic*. Vols. I, II. Oxford, 1911.

————, *The Meeting of Extremes in Contemporary Philosophy*. London, 1921.

Bradley, Francis Herbert, *Appearance and Reality*. A metaphysical essay. London, 1920.

————, *The Principles of Logic*, London, 1928.

————, *Collected Essays*. Oxford, 1935.

————, *Ethical Studies*. Oxford, 1935.

————, *Essays on Truth and Reality*. Oxford, 1944.

Breton, Stanislas, *L' "Esse In" et L' "Esse Ad" Dans la Métaphysique de la Relation*. Rome, 1951.

Caird, Edward, *Hegel*. London, 1883.

Cresson, Andre, *Hegel. Sa Vie, Son Oeuvre*. Paris, 1949.

Dürr, Agnes, *Zum Problem der Hegelschen Dialektik und ihrer Formen*. Berlin, 1938.

Dulkeit, Gerhard, *Die Idee Gottes im Geiste der Philosophie Hegels*. Munich, 1947.

Fessard, Gaston, *Deux interprètes de la Phénoménologie de Hegel*: Jean Hyppolite et Alexandre Kojève: Etudes 1947, p. 368 ff.

Findlay, J. N., *Hegel. A Re-examination*. Muirhead Library of Philosophy. London, 1958.

Fischer, Kuno, *Hegels Leben, Werke, Lehre*: Geschichte der Neueren Philosophie. 8. Bd. Heidelberg, 1911.

Gauss, Hermann, *Uber die Bedeutung und Grenzen des dialektischen Prinzips in der Philosophie (Platon und Hegel)*: Zeitschr. f. phil. Forschung. 5 (1961), 321 ff.

Geiger, L. B. *La Participation Dans La Philosophie de S. Thomas d'Aquin*. Paris, 1953.

Gellner, Ernest, *Words and Things*, with Forward by Bertrand Russell. London, 1959.

Glockner, Hermann, *Hegel*. Vols. I, II (Jubilee Edition, nos. 21, 22). Stuttgart, 1929.

————, *Der Begriff in Hegels Philosophie*. Tübingen, 1924.

Grégoire, Franz, *Hegel et la primauté respective de la raison et du rationnel*. Revue neoscolastique de philosophie, 1940-1945, t. 43, pp. 252-264.

————, *Hegel et l'universelle contradiction*: Revue phil. de Louvain 44 (1946) 36 ff.

————, *Aux sources de la pensée de Marx, Hegel, Feuerbach*. Louvain, 1947.

————, *La dialectique hégélienne de l'être, du néant et du devenir*. Revue de Métaphysique et Morale, 1957, no. 1, pp. 84-95.

————, *Thèmes hégéliens et dépassements d'inspiration thomiste*. Sapientia Aquinatis. Communications IV Congressus thomistici internationalis, Romae, 1955, pp. 252-291.

————, *Essai d'une phénoménologie des preuves métaphysique de Dieu*. Louvain, 1955.

————, *Études hégéliennes*. Les Points Capitaux du Système. Louvain, 1958.

Haering, Theodor, *Hegel sein Wollen und sein Werk*. Vol. I, II. Leipzig, 1929.

Haldane, R. B. H., *The Reign of Relativity*. London, 1921.

Hartmann, Albert, *Der Spätidealismus und die Hegelsche Dialektik*. Berlin, 1937.

Hartmann, Nicolai, *Die Philosophie des deutschen Idealismus*. Vol. I, II Berlin-Leipzig, 1929.

————, *Aristoteles und Hegel*. Erfurt, 1933.

————, *Hegel und das Problem der Realdialektik*. Bl. f. dt. Phil. (1935/36) 1, ff.

Hegel, G. W. F., *Complete Works*. Jubilee Edition, ed. Glockner, Stuttgart 1927-1930.

Heidegger, Martin, *Sein und Zeit*, I. Halle, 1941.

————, *Vom Wesen der Wahrheit*. Frankfort. 1949.

————, *Platons Lehre von der Wahrheit*. Berne, 1947.

————, *Was ist Metaphysik?* Frankfort, 1949.

Heimann, Betty, *System und Methode in Hegels Philosophie*, Leipzig, 192.

Heiss, Robert, *Das Verhältnis Von Theorie und Praxis bei Hegel*. Bl. f. d Phil. 9 (1935/36), 75 ff.

Horvath, Alexander, *Metaphysik der Relationen*. Graz, 1914.

Hötchl, Calixt, *Das Absolute in Hegels Dialektik, sein Wesen und sei Aufgabe*. Paderborn, 1941.

Hyppolite, Jean, *Genèse et structure de la Phénoménologie de l'Esprit Hegel*. Paris, 1946.

————, *Introduction a la philosophie de l'histoire de Hegel*. Paris, 194

————, *Études sur Marx et Hegel*. Paris, 1955.

Jansen, Bernhard, *Dialektische oder Akt-Potenz-Metaphysik*, Hegel-renaissance oder Hegelkritik? Aufstiege zur Metaphysik. Freiburg i. Br. 1933.

Kojève, Alexandre, *Introduction à la lecture de Hegel*. Lecons sur la Phénoménologie de l'Esprit. Paris, 1947.

Krempel, A. *La Doctrine de la Relation Chez Saint Thomas* Paris, 1952.

Kroner, Richard, *Von Kant bis Hegel*. Vol. I, II. Tubingen, 1924.

————, *Hegel sum 100. Todestage*. Tubingen, 1932.

Kuiper, Vincent M., *Hegels Denken. Die Erhebung zum speculativen Standpunkt*. Rome, 1931.

————, *Le "Réalisme" de Hegel*. Revue des Sciences, Tom. XX, pp. 233 ff.

Lasson, George, *Beitrage zur Hegelforschung*. Berlin, 1909.

Lossky, *Hegel als Intuitivist*. Bl. f. dt. Phil. 9 1935/36) pp. 62 ff.

Maréchal, Joseph, *Le point de départ de la metaphysique*. Paris-Brussels, 1923-1926.

May, Rollo, *Existence*. New York, 1958.

Metzke, E., *Hegels Vorreden mit Kommentar*. Eine Einfuhrung in sinee Philosophie. Heidelberg, 1949.

Moller, Josef, *Der Geist und das Absolute*. Zur Grundlegung einer Religionsphilosophie in Begegnung mit Hegels Denkwelt. Paderborn, 1951.

McTaggart, John, *Studies in Hegelian Dialectic*. Cambridge 1896.

————, *Studies in Hegelian Cosmology*. London, 1918.

————, *Philosophical Studies*. London, 1934.

Niel, Henri, *De la médiation dans la philosophie de Hegel*. Paris, 1945.

Nink, Casper, *Kommentar zu den grundlegenden Abschnitten von Hegels Phänomenologie des Geistes*. Regensburg, 1931.

————, *Die Grundlage der Philosophie Hegels*. Eine kritische Untersuchung. Phil. Jahrb. 44 (1931) pp. 171 ff.

Noel, G., *La Logique de Hegel*. Paris, 1897.

Przywara, Erich, *Thomas und Hegel*: Ringen der Gegenwart II, Augsburg, 1929, pp. 930 ff.

Rovighi, S. Vanni, *Hegel critico di Kant*. Rivista de filos. neo-scolastica. 42 (1950) pp. 289 ff.

Sartre, Jean-Paul, *L'Etre et le néant*. Paris, 1943.

Schilling-Wollny, Kurt, *Hegels Wissenschaft von der Wirklichkeit und ihre Quellen I*. Munich, 1929.

Sesemann, W., *Zum Problem der Dialaktik*. Bl. f. dt. Phil. 9 (1935/36), pp. 28 ff.

Stace, W. T., *The Philosophy of Hegel*. London, 1924.

Steinbuchel, Theodor, *Das Grundproblem der Hegelschen Philosophie I*. Bonn, 1923.

———, *Wesen, Welt und Grenze des deutschen Idealismus*. Eine Rechenschaftsablage zu Hegels 100 Todestage. Phil. Jahrb. 44 (1931), pp. 289. ff.

Wahl, Jean, *Le malheur de la conscience dans la philosophie de Hegel*. Paris, 1929.

Wallace, William, *The Logic of Hegel*. London, 1873.

———, *Prolegomena to Hegel's Philosophy of Mind*. London, 1892.

Welte, Bernard, *Hegels Begriff der Religion—sein Sinn und seine Grenze*. Scholastik 27 (1952), pp. 210 ff.

Werkmeister, W. H., *A History of Philosophical Ideas in America*, New York, 1949.

Wigersma, B., *Verhandlungen des ersten, zweiten und dritten Hegelkongresses* (1930 u. 1933), 3 Bde. Tubingen-Haarlem, 1931-1934.

Willmann, Otto, *Geschichte des Idealismus*. Braunschweig, 1907.